THE BRITISH ACADEMY

The Relations between the Laws of Babylonia and the Laws of the Hebrew Peoples

By

The Rev. C. H. W. Johns, M.A., Litt.D.

Master of St. Catharine's College, Cambridge

The Schweich Lectures

1912

THE BRITISH ACADEMY

The Relations between the Laws of Babylonia and the Laws of the Hebrew Peoples

By

The Rev. C. H. W. Johns, M.A., Litt.D.

Master of St. Catharine's College, Cambridge

The Schweich Lectures

1912

WIPF & STOCK · Eugene, Oregon

Wipf and Stock Publishers
199 W 8th Ave, Suite 3
Eugene, OR 97401

The Relations between the Laws of Babylonia
and the Laws of the Hebrew Peoples
The Schweich Lectures 1912
By Johns, C. H. W.
ISBN 13: 978-1-4982-8810-1
Publication date 2/2/2016
Previously published by Kraus-thomson
Organization GmbH. Munchen, 1912

PREFACE

It has long been held that the laws of the Israelites, as revealed by God to Moses, by him embodied in the books of the Pentateuch and since preserved by the zealous care of the Jewish people, are incomparable. Accordingly they have been adopted professedly by most Christian nations and were early accepted by our own king Alfred [1] as the basis of the law system of this our land.

We live in an age of devotion to comparative methods, when it is an article of faith to hold that the most fruitful means to attain a clear understanding of the exact nature of anything is to compare it with its like. This comparative method forms a large part of modern scientific research and, with proper safeguards and reserves, has become a favourite weapon of literary research into the history of human institutions.

Long ago, as it seems to us, Sir Henry Maine used it [2] when he wrote his *History of Early Law*. As a consequence of his investigations and those of many who have followed in his footsteps, the Science of Comparative Law has grown up. All the great law systems of the world have been classified and compared, and comparative lawyers felt qualified to assign to any new-found fragment of ancient law its true position in their schemes. The results had rather confirmed than traversed ancient claims for the supremacy of Mosaic Laws. Men had settled down to the belief that we might compare, and that to its great advantage, the Legislation of Moses with the Roman Laws of the XII Tables, with the Indian Laws of Manu or the Greek Code of Gortyna. We had recognized the broad outlines of a process of evolution and begun to understand the way in which, as a people advanced along the path of progress in the elements of civilization, similar human needs called forth similar solutions of the questions of right and wrong.

Nevertheless much remained obscure in many ancient legislations. It was the opinion of Jhering,[3] the great authority on Roman Law, that for the ultimate solution of the puzzles of Roman Law we should have to go back to Babylon. In his days comparatively little was known about the laws of Babylonia, and that little was badly attested. Men were still of opinion that the Mosaic Law was the oldest of which

we had any trustworthy account and that Babylonian laws, if there
ever were any worthy of the name, must have been more barbarous
and unformed.

Then there came, in the early days of this century, a great surprise, calling at once for much revision of our neatly arranged systems
of knowledge. A Code of Laws was discovered, certainly the oldest
known, by far the most complete and best attested, and at the same
time the most advanced of all but the most modern.

Fragments of it were already known from late copies, had been
recognized as probably parts of a Babylonian Code of Law, were even
conjecturally styled the Code of Hammurabi by PROFESSOR FRIEDRICH
DELITZSCH,[4] but very little could be concluded from them. Then
suddenly at Susa in Elam was discovered practically the whole text
of it. Ever since it has been the subject of profound study from all
points of view.

The comparison of this Code of Hammurabi with the Laws of
Moses was bound to be made. Many reasons would suggest the like-
lihood that much similarity would be observed between two early
legislations both Semitic in complexion. Comparisons with other
ancient codes were equally sure to be made and the differences
naturally to be expected would be carefully weighed and considered.
But while most surprising results came out of these comparisons,
especially in the realm of Roman Law, a much keener interest has
attached to the comparison with Hebrew Law, not only because of the
sacred nature of the Old Testament, but even more because this had
been the special study of the Higher Critics. These scholars had
almost decided what their view of the composition of the Pentateuch
should be, what were the ultimate sources implied, what dates should
be assigned to the constituent documents, and the arguments to be
considered valid in such discussions. Those who rejected the Higher
Critical conclusions flew at once to the new-found Code for arguments
to refute Higher Criticism ; while Higher Critics found confirmations
in many directions.

It may be hoped that this side issue has lost its interest, and that
a hearing may now be obtained for a simple attempt to use the two
legislations for mutual understanding. When on the appearance of
the Code in its first edition I lectured upon it at Queens' College,
Cambridge, it was solely as a new document of human history. When
a month or two later I was privileged to point out its 'significance
for comparison with the Hebrew legislation' in a paper read before
the Cambridge Theological Society,[5] of which an abstract appeared in
the *Journal of Theological Studies* (Jan. 1903), it is probable enough

that the contrasts to the Mosaic Law were more apparent than the likenesses. In the next few months there was ready for press an extensive work on the Code, illustrating its meaning from the innumerable legal documents, most of them contemporary, which had been my study for years. As bearing on this comparison I soon found that a baldly literal translation of the Code gave a most Biblical turn to its phraseology which the easy, lucid, but paraphrastic renderings given by others perpetually disguised. The general likenesses, Semitic characteristics, and apparent cases of adaptation were separately classed and those most suggestive of dependence insisted upon. The index of subjects compiled from the Code and contemporary legal documents appeared to constitute a substantial advance in the knowledge of ancient law.

Of all this work, prepared in 1904, it was not possible to publish more than the translation, under the title *The Oldest Code of Laws in the World* (T. & T. Clark, Edinburgh), with a selection from the index. The other results were freely communicated to various scholars, but it was not without some pangs that I saw most of them attained in time independently. Later an article on the *Code of Hammurabi* in the Supplementary Volume of Hastings's *Bible Dictionary* and one on *Babylonian Law* in the *Encyclopaedia Britannica* afforded me the chance of setting out some results of my research upon the Code in its relation to the ancient civilization of Babylonia, with a rapid glance at its relations to Israelite Law. When writing a work for the American public on *Assyrian and Babylonian Laws, Contracts, and Letters*, I expanded some parts of this treatment.

I trust that I may be pardoned for thus simply stating why, when the British Academy conferred upon me the great honour of inviting me to deliver the Schweich Lectures for 1912, I selected the subject of *Babylonian Law in its relation to the Laws of Moses*. It was a subject in which I had taken an interest for some years, and I was anxious to seize an opportunity of making public the work done in 1903-4.

A very large amount of work has been done by others on various aspects of the Code of Hammurabi, especially on the Continent, where the facilities for publication appear to be greatly superior to those in England. What is done here is, however, of excellent quality ; and Mr. S. A. Cook undertook a detailed comparison with the laws of Hammurabi and other codes which[6] leaves very little to be desired. Mr. St. Chad Boscawen in his *First of Empires* stated some interesting opinions, and Mr. Chilperic Edwards has given a fresh translation. Professor R. F. Harper gave a useful handbook of the text with new translation, index, vocabulary, sign-list, &c., which makes the study simple to those who can read cuneiform.

Reference may be made to the Bibliographies given in these and other books listed in the Bibliography printed on pp. 65 ff.

With such a volume of literature already published, it may seem superfluous to add a further contribution. Indeed, when the present writer read an account of the Code to the Cambridge Theological Society in October 1902, he was quite content to call his paper *The Code of Hammurabi, fresh material for comparison with the Mosaic Code.* He would have been well content to leave it as such, being rather concerned to furnish material for study than to make direct contributions to the application of it to subjects beyond his competence. Much that has been published on this comparison, however, seems to him really inadequate or so ill-considered that it appears to be a duty to submit a different view. He is fully conscious that it is only one view and may prove to be wrong. Yet it seems to him that it is a view which takes account of more facts than any other, and, while not admitting of formal proof, is both reasonable and probable.

Briefly stated, the view thus taken is that the Code of Hammurabi belongs to the same group of ancient legislations as the Hebrew, and that both are compromises between two distinct types of law.

One type is that which is perhaps best seen in the customs of the Arabs, as still surviving among the modern Bedawin, and known to us from the ancient Arabic writers. This has been called primitive Semitic custom. The Israelites, before their entrance into Canaan, as a nomad pastoral people, would be governed by such law, if it can be called law. The dynasty to which Hammurabi belonged was foreign to Babylonia. It owed its rise to an incursion of a Semitic people. That Semites were in Babylonia long before is true, but this was a fresh invasion by a probably nomad pastoral race. They had previously obeyed the same primitive laws as it is assumed the Israelites did before their settlement in Canaan. Forming as they did the ruling race in Babylonia, they yet clung with Oriental conservatism to their ancient customs. Even such a powerful ruler as Hammurabi could not, or at any rate did not see fit to, entirely change those customs. In the period when the Laws of Moses were instituted, the Israelites were similarly the ruling race in Canaan. Their earlier laws, as known to us, show the same conservation of primitive custom, and that of the same type.

The other type of law is that due to a settled community. In Babylonia it may have been evolved through long ages. It may have been, and probably was, largely due to a non-Semitic people, usually called Sumerians, whose racial affinities are not yet well made out. These were conquered by the Semites of Hammurabi's race. In Canaan too the invading Israelites found a long-settled people in possession. They were governed by very similar laws to those of the settled Babylonians. That these laws had been imported from Babylonia is open to question. Much that is common to the laws of the two settled communities may have arisen independently. There is as yet no evidence that the Canaanites were of the Sumerian stock.[7] But Babylonian influence on the Canaanite law is quite conceivable, and is supported by historical evidence of long-continued intercourse between Babylonia and the West. As the Israelites became a settled population many of their nomad customs must have become inappropriate. They might have evolved new laws. They might have taken over the laws of the Canaanites, so far as these were innocent, or not too obnoxious to Hebrew prejudices. Exactly which course they followed in each case is matter of history. The historical evidence may be inconclusive. We must make the best of it.

When, therefore, the Code of Hammurabi is compared with the Laws of Moses, the common material may be due to one of two common sources, primitive Semitic law (otherwise nomad law) and the law of settled communities. For the latter we may hesitate to fix on a racial name. But it is not necessarily that of any and every settled community. Inasmuch as we find it in its most developed form in the Code of Hammurabi, we may call it Babylonian. On the other hand, as the oldest known witness to the primitive type is the same Code, we may call that Babylonian also. In this modified sense we shall be able to speak of the Laws of Moses as being primitive Semitic law modified by Babylonian influence. That, however, would be a description easily misunderstood if divorced from its context.

It is better to say that both legislations are compromises between the two types of law, that they show different degrees of preponderance of one or the other type, and that the Laws of Moses manifest an independent development strongly influenced by the Code of Hammurabi.

We may still claim an independent development of the Laws of Moses.

For during the whole time that the Israelites were in Canaan they were, as usually supposed, independent of Babylonian rule. If they adopted laws which were already prevalent in Babylonia, we may be sure it was not solely because they were Babylonian. This may be disputed. For there were times when, if we may believe their own tradition, they did receive embassies from Babylonia, or even adopt

Assyrian cults. This kind of influence might conceivably lead to the adoption of Babylonian or Assyrian law, which latter was always practically the Code of Hammurabi.

The Israelites may never have adopted Canaanite law consciously, but always supposed themselves to be creators of their own laws. But they could hardly avoid knowing the Canaanite law. When a man does as his neighbours do, he may be perfectly independent in his choice so to do, as some men count independence. But it is usual to regard him as influenced by their conduct. Even when he decides to do the very opposite to what they do we may contend that he was influenced by his knowledge of their conduct. Reaction may be claimed as a sign of independence, but it is also a sign of influence. The truth always is that every action exhibits both independence and influence. We may hold to the explanation that a man's circumstances determine him, but we must then give a wide meaning to circumstance.

Now one of Israel's circumstances was Canaan. The Canaanites had settled laws, and to some extent those laws must have embodied the results of experience of what was suitable in Canaan. Israel might have arrived at the same results, by the same way. It is, however, surely difficult to deny that they availed themselves of Canaanite experience and adopted Canaanite laws. If they did so at all, it is mere quibbling to deny Canaanite influence. Even if they had so framed their laws as to avoid a likeness to Canaanite laws altogether, that would still show Canaanite influence. That they did neither, but achieved a totally distinct type of law, can alone show complete independence. That they did not adopt all Canaanite customs, but made a selection, shows the best sort of independence. That there was always a strong tendency to adopt too much that was Canaanite, is the lament of their best teachers. These also protested against much that was Israelite custom. But it is not certain that these protests were always against what had been Canaanite. It may sometimes have been more primitive custom, properly more Israelite. For, at any rate, regarded from the point of civilization, we must admit that the Canaanites were more advanced.

It might now be supposed that the differences of opinion which have been called forth by comparisons of the Hebrew and Babylonian legislations resolve themselves into this : that one opinion emphasizes the independence, the other dwells upon the influence. That is partly true, but does not cover all the divergence. For when similarities are accounted for by a common Semitic origin, or an *Urgesetz*, or as the natural outcome of human intellect acting similarly in similar circumstances, not all the factors of the problem are taken into account. These might be adequate solutions if Israel had been separated from all other Semitic races and entered an empty Canaan. They might even account for the similarities, such as they are, between the laws of the Babylonians and the Aztecs. Men everywhere do reach the invention of pottery, but man anywhere will use the pot he finds ready made.

What these contentions leave out of account is the existence of ready-made laws. This cannot be denied. The Canaanites were there, by all admitted. They must have had laws and customs. No one surely denies that. What proof could ever be produced that Israel did not adopt such as were convenient? In the selections and rejections which the Israelites made they showed whatever independence we may give them credit for. That they could have invented the same themselves, or obtained them elsewhere, is perfectly irrelevant. To assert that they did invent them, not adopt them, is to describe the same fact in different words. It looks very like perversity. We may pretend to have invented something exactly like what some one else has done before, but the Patent Laws usually prevent our getting much profit out of it. Even when we introduce judicious little variations there is sometimes astonishing reluctance to credit us with the inventiveness which we feel to be our own.

Some writers have boldly gone to the root of the matter and minimized the extent to which Canaan was influenced by Babylonia. This is perfectly legitimate. We cannot be too cautious how we use the facts of history. Eastern lands show to-day that the tide of conquest may roll over them and leave little trace behind. Egypt was influential in Palestine once, but there is not much trace of its influence in Canaan. This, however, is not entirely absent. Explorations in Palestine do exhibit considerable traces of Egyptian influence in some directions. What traces of Israelite influence are there to compare with it? Here, however, the question is being taken into a totally irrelevant field.

The Canaanites adopted exactly what suited them, they submitted to what was imposed, just so long as they were obliged. That they adopted all the Babylonian laws is absurd to suppose. Just as absurd as to suppose that under Israelite rule, they adopted all Israelite law or custom. If they had, there would then be nothing left for Israel to select or reject. Let us give them credit for some independence even when conquered. Their law was a Canaanite version of Babylonian or Israelite law, in any case. If they had it written down in cuneiform even, it was probably translated into Canaanite. Some would maintain that that was Hebrew. At any rate, what we know of it is very similar. But that they could have escaped Babylonian influence on their laws is almost inconceivable. What we know of the Laws of Moses either proves that they were, in some cases, practically the same as Babylonian, or else shows direct Babylonian influence. We may turn this evidence the other way and say that the Code of Hammurabi shows Canaanite influence, from what we can see in it to be like the Laws of Moses. There are not lacking some to call the dynasty of Hammurabi 'Canaanite'. But the evidence rather goes to show that what Hammurabi's race contributed to his Code was more like what Israel contributed to the Laws of Moses and not at all like what a settled folk, such as the Canaanites, would contribute. We may perhaps concede that the Canaanites were Semitic and of the same race as those who conquered Babylon and founded Hammurabi's Dynasty. At that time they may have been nomads, as the Israelites were later when they came into Canaan. But if, in Canaan, they retained a primitive type of law and evolved a settled law or adopted it from some previous inhabitants, so that their law also, like the Code of Hammurabi and the Laws of Moses, was a blend of the two types; then we have no longer the means to separate their particular blend from the other two.

It is of great importance to discern what was Canaanite law, and we shall find some traces of it. But on the whole, we can only infer it by separating from Israelite law what they are likely to have contributed to it. It is not a very safe method, but we have no other yet. Some contributions are made by the Tell-el-Amarna tablets. More may be expected from fresh discoveries. There is another indirect method. The laws of Phoenicia and Carthage may give some help. Even the Roman Laws of the XII Tables may be of use. They do show surprising likenesses to the Code of Hammurabi. How these laws could find their way from Babylonia to Rome is not easy to imagine. Phoenicia may be thought of as an intermediary. If this be tolerated as a solution, then we may assume that where Babylon agrees with Rome, especially if Phoenicia can be shown to agree also, it is probable that Canaan was also very similar. If then Israel is the same as well we can hardly doubt whence the original motive came.

There are possibly some indications that the Laws of Moses mark an advance on the customs which ruled in the days of the Patriarchs. In view of modern critical contentions that these stories of the Patriarchs are a sort of reflection back into the past of what the later writers felt would be appropriate to the time in which they set the eponymous heroes of the old days, we may hesitate to regard such attributed customs as trustworthy for a comparison. Nor is it beyond question whether the Israelites ever obeyed the laws of Bedouin Arabs. But assuming that on their entrance into Canaan the Israelites acquired fresh customs, we may make some important reflections. Supposing there was a change in law, can we detect it? If we can, what exactly does it establish? Have we merely a change due to a change of habitat, or have other factors to be taken into account?

Now we may question whether this change of law was due to the change in habits from a nomadic life to a settled state, simply and solely. The Israelites when they invaded Canaan found there an already settled people, if we may believe their own account. There were cities and houses and crops already there. From secular sources, such as the Tell-el-Amarna tablets, we know that some time before the conquest there was an advanced state of civilization in Canaan. We even know the names of many kings and cities. What became of this settled population? It is contrary to all analogy and to the Israelite tradition itself to suppose that they were all exterminated. They were obviously possessed of a higher civilization than their invaders, already, what the Israelites in time became, a settled people. Can it be thought that they exerted no influence on their conquerors? We cannot but expect that as the Israelites became settled they would adopt the customs of the settled population. We have it on record that their own teachers charged them with doing this. Some of these customs must have been innocent enough, and such as would be equally appropriate for Israelites when settled. Others would be obnoxious to the racial prejudices, religious or social, of the more conservative Israelites. There would naturally be conflict in some cases between conflicting views of right. In some cases one view would prevail, in others a different result would follow. Even compromises are not inconceivable. To insist that all laws in Israel were the product of the national genius, even if dignified by the name of revelation, is to make a heavy demand on our credulity.

It seems then to be a reasonable working hypothesis that the Israelites did at first succeed in impressing a primitive type of law on the land, especially in those matters which were not entirely unsuited to both peoples. This seems to be supported by the character of what is regarded as the earliest law code in Israel. We at any rate may say that they themselves regarded such as their laws. It would require strong proof before we could admit that the surviving conquered people obeyed them too. As the Israelites became a settled people they may have invented fresh laws. It does require proof, however, that these were invented, and not already the laws of the conquered race. Provided that they were not too repugnant to the Hebrew genius it would be a step towards unification to adopt existing laws. Proof must be overwhelming that they were not adopted before we can think otherwise. The selective power to adopt or reject, to modify and concede, completely guards independence. On the other hand, unless we can prove that there was no adoption at all, we admit influence. Here the controversialists seem to have confounded the issue. They either deny all influence in order to maintain independence, or they destroy all independence by hardening influence into origination. On either assumption Moses does not get credit for much initiative.

Hitherto we have not considered the question whether the settled Canaanites were governed by the Code of Hammurabi before the Israelites came. Some have tried to make the whole controversy turn on this point. It is difficult to see how an answer can be given to that question, except by the discovery of a copy of the Code itself in a pre-Israelitish city. If, on the other hand, we admit that the civilization of Canaan was essentially Babylonian before the conquest, we may suppose that it was governed by Babylonian laws, at any rate, to a large extent. It is to be expected that there would be local variations. Can we test such an hypothesis? We do now know what Babylonian law was in the time of Hammurabi some five hundred years before the conquest of Canaan. We do know that in Babylonia that law remained practically unchanged for a thousand years longer. We must then admit that if Babylonian law had sway in Canaan at all, it must have been that of the Code to all intents and purposes. We thus have a linked chain of hypotheses. If Canaanite civilization was once an offshoot of Babylonian, and gradually asserted its influence over Hebrew legislation, then we ought to find more and more likeness to the Code of Hammurabi in Israelite law as time goes on. For that purpose we may concede as much as the critics wish to claim for their arrangement of successive codes in the Books of Moses before the Code was discovered. The later the law is, according to them, the more likely will it be on our hypothesis to resemble the Code. We assume that the Canaanite element in the nation held on to their old law, while submitting to the innovations introduced by the invaders. If the other proposition holds true, either this was the fact, or the particular law, instead of being late, must be redated before Canaanite conservatism was overcome.

We may now state the broad principle to be tested. The more primitive laws in the Mosaic Codes are properly Israelite, and an inheritance from old nomadic custom. The more advanced laws are due to gradually assimilated Canaanite sources. These should show, if not identity, at least affinity with the Code of Hammurabi. If they do not, we have several alternative views to weigh. Either the law of Hammurabi did not continue to bear sway in Canaan, or it never did on that point, or the law is a new creation. The mere fact that a given, late, non-primitive law in Israel is not found in the Code of Hammurabi proves nothing as to the origin of any unconnected law. We have to do with a long chain, of which we can only compare the two ends. What happened between we do not know.

We may do well to clear out of the way some obstacles that might at least distract attention. An apparently strong point has been made against any connexion between the legislations on the score of philology. It is said that while the names of the things dealt with are the same, the technical terms are different. Thus, while the words for silver and gold, sheep and oxen, fields and houses are the same, those for rulers, for laws and customs are different. This is partly an argument from silence, partly an ignoration of facts. It is true that 'to marry', in Babylonian, is *aḥâzu*, and in Hebrew *lāḳâh*; but in Assyrian it is *laḳû*. Now we may reply that the Assyrian shows that it was once *laḳû* in Babylonian also. The connexion for which we contend does not demand transliteration, but translation. What would be thought of any student of mediaeval history who denied the influence of Roman law on English because Latin words were not used? If this be the test, the Tell-el-Amarna tablets show much stronger Babylonian influence than we contend for. Practically the whole of their vocabulary is Babylonian. They also show that the writers had words of their own, Semitic, if not Hebrew, which they glossed by Babylonian. Some think the Israelites learnt their Hebrew in Canaan. If the Canaanites were speaking Hebrew and had Babylonian laws, the translating into Hebrew was done before the conquest. The fact is that the whole philological argument breaks down unless we can show that the words compared are the only words in use with the same meaning. The lexicons do not on the whole afford a sufficient source for the comparison. They embody little of the vocabulary of the legal documents or contracts.

Of much more cogency than the agreement of separate items would be a similarity of order in the arrangement of the common matter. PROFESSOR D. H. MÜLLER has found some interesting examples of this in comparing the Code with the Twelve Tables. This leads him and

others to suspect an Oriental influence on early Roman Law. That must remain little more than a suspicion unless we can indicate the route by which such influence could come in. In the case of Israel the problem is to show how it could be kept out.

A comparison of the Code with the Laws of Moses from this point of view is greatly hampered by the fact that the latter are not in any particular order. If we follow the critical division of the material we find that we are left with a variety of legislations of very different dates and qualities well shown in *The Hexateuch*, or in articles in *Dict. Bible*. It will hardly be claimed for any one of these that we have it still in a completely preserved form. If so, then the intention must have been to leave a great deal to the action of the well-known customary law.

This solution, however, is not to be rejected off-hand. For the Code of Hammurabi does not deal expressly with all cases: it omits murder. Hence we must not insist that any Israelite code either, when first promulgated, covered all cases of crime and misdemeanour. There is, however, good ground for saying that each Israelite legislation included some things which are now omitted from the Books of Moses. If this be denied, then we must account for the very incomplete nature of these codes. We may do so thus. It was only to be expected that a new legislation would deal chiefly with cases that had not hitherto been decided, or on which old law had grown obsolete, or where conflicting views of right had come to be held. If, then, we can regard any Israelite code, as now known to us, as being on the whole preserved in its original order, even though other portions have been suppressed or abrogated, we may compare the order of its clauses with those of the Code of Hammurabi. We need not take account of the suspicions which will now be thrown on that order by critics, unless they were expressed before the Code of Hammurabi was known. And on the whole case we may plead with respect to any Israelite code, that either it once covered much more than it does, as we know it now, or that its incompleteness is due to the existence of well-established custom on the omitted points, and that it simply enacted changes.

As a result of the intensive work done on the Code of Hammurabi itself by the many scholars who have devoted their study to it, we now understand it far better than before. It would be invidious to attempt to assign each step to its own author, and I expressly disclaim any originality for views that I may have held long before some one else published them, but it may add to the confidence with which my readers follow me, if they remember that nearly everything has been independently reached by two students at least. My chief desire, however, is to make my views clear, and to state my reasons as intelligibly as may be.

I propose to deal first with the external features of the Code of Hammurabi, dwelling chiefly on those that are useful for a comparison with the Israelite legislation. Then, secondly, I will point out briefly the types of likeness between the Babylonian and Hebrew laws, and the associated contrasts. Then I will venture to discuss in my way and attempt to estimate the extent of dependence, if any. But I cannot claim to have said the last word on any point raised here. We are still at the mercy of future discovery. Let us hope it will be merciful to some theories, at any rate.

THE RELATIONS BETWEEN THE LAWS OF BABYLONIA AND THE LAWS OF THE HEBREW PEOPLES

LECTURE I

THE discovery of the principal record of the system of enactments now known by the name of the Code of Hammurabi was made in December 1901 and January 1902.

At Susa, the ancient Persepolis, named 'Shushan the Palace' in the Book of Daniel, situated in Persia, once the ancient capital of Elam, the excavators, working under the direction of J. de Morgan for the French Ministry of Instruction, found three large pieces of black diorite, which when fitted together formed a monolith stela, about 2·25 metres high, tapering upwards from 1·9 to 1·65 metres. The stone itself is in the Louvre Museum in Paris, but a beautiful reproduction of it stands in the Babylonian Room of the British Museum.

At the top of the stela is engraved in low bas-relief a representation of Hammurabi himself receiving his laws from a seated god, usually taken to be the sun-god Shamash, who was regarded in Babylonia as the supreme judge of gods and men, whose children or attendants were Mishâru and Kittu or Rectitude and Right.

Below this scene begins the inscription, written in Semitic Babylonian, then called Akkadian, and arranged in parallel narrow columns. These columns were read from left to right and downward precisely like those of a modern newspaper, but each column goes across the stela like a belt. Consequently a reader must turn his head on one side to read the inscription.

On the front of the stela sixteen columns are preserved, and traces of five more which have been intentionally erased. Analogy with similar cases among the many Babylonian monuments found at Susa, on which the original inscription has been partly cut out to make way for the name and titles of Shutruk-nakhunde the king of Elam who had carried them off as trophies of his conquests in Babylonia, suggests that a like purpose was entertained with respect to this stela but only partly carried out. Unfortunately a break in the text of the Code is thus caused which our other records have only partly enabled us to restore.

B

The back of the stela completely preserves twenty-eight columns, except where a few natural faults in the stone obscure the characters. The whole inscription may be estimated as having once contained forty-nine columns, four thousand lines, and about eight thousand words.

The characters are of an archaic type, much fancied by the kings of the First Dynasty of Babylon, of whom Hammurabi was the sixth in succession, and paralleled by other inscriptions of his. Thus, apart from his own words, we can date it as a contemporary record of the text. It was undoubtedly engraved on the stone by a stone-cutter working from a copy of the text written on clay in the cursive script of the period. This accounts for one or two scribal errors, which are, however, easily detected and readily corrected.

Fragments of duplicates were also found at Susa, showing that the text was executed in several copies, probably to be set up in different cities. At least one fragment of a contemporary copy written on clay was found at Nippur, showing that the text was also circulated in writing at the time of its promulgation.

There are fragments of several copies preserved in the British Museum, made for the Library of Ashurbânipal, king of Assyria 668–626 B.C. These are in Assyrian script and show some variants which are useful as synonymous renderings. From their phraseology, however, Dr. Br. Meissner, who first published most of them, concluded that they were early Babylonian laws,[7] while Professor Friedrich Delitzsch, who commented upon them, named them the Code of Hammurabi.[8] Further, a late Babylonian copy exists at Berlin, and was published by Dr. F. E. Peiser.[9]

These late copies show that the inscription was edited in a series of tablets or 'Books' called *Ninu Anum tsirum*, from the first words of the text, just as Genesis was called Bereshith from its first word or other books of the Old Testament were named in the same way. Another series was called *Dinâni sha Hammurabi*, from the first words of the Epilogue or closing portion of the text. From these editions we may conclude that the Code was known and studied both in Assyria and Babylonia at least as late as the seventh century B.C. Whether any monumental stela with this inscription survived so long after the Susa examples had been carried off is not yet certain. But these editions are of extreme value as indications that a knowledge of the provisions of the Code existed so long and was preserved so accurately.

We may note that there is a very great advantage for students of this ancient body of law in the fact that beside a long tradition accurately preserved we have a practically complete autograph of the Code as originally promulgated. There can be no suspicion of over-writing, interpolation or gloss, no tendency-redaction, no revision in the interests of any party, priestly or political. We have no need to seek for any conjectural restoration, except for a few erased clauses or defaced characters. We have no call to split up the text[10] into strata as embodying older laws, though we know such earlier codes had existed perhaps a thousand years before. A comparison with such fragments of earlier law as we possess shows indeed much change if not always progress in that period, and marks on the whole a great advance in civilization.

It is a task still reserved for the students of Babylonian law to make careful researches into the growth of social institutions and the development of legal conceptions which led up to this Code. It will prove a most instructive study if pursued apart from the presumptions deduced from other and unrelated areas which now form a body of dogmatic prejudice from which many scholars seem unable to emancipate their thought. We must, however, start our investigations at a point where the Code has already arrived, when it must be treated as the principal landmark in the long history of law in Babylonia. Whatever may be our view as to what should have been the evolution of law before that date we must be careful to remember what that evolution produced.

The date of the Code, as shown by the prologue with which the text begins, fell in the reign[11] of the great king Hammurabi, sixth king of the First Dynasty of Babylon, whose call to the throne, successful wars, and great benefits to his people, it sets out with magniloquent phraseology. The list of his achievements thus given further enables us to fix the year of its redaction as after the fortieth year of the reign. This may, however, be the date at which our existing monument was erected rather than that at which the Code was first promulgated. As this king only reigned forty-three years the date is very closely fixed. We now know some prominent event for each year of this long reign, and by means of other inscriptions of his we can make out a fairly complete sketch of his times for which reference must be made to the many excellent histories of Babylonia.[12] As is well known Hammurabi has frequently been identified with Amraphel king of Shinar mentioned in the fourteenth chapter of Genesis as having made war on his rebellious subjects in and around the Dead Sea area. Amraphel is there associated with Arioch king of Ellasar, usually identified with Rîm-Sin king of Larsa, with Chedorlaomer king of Elam and Tidal king of ' Nations'. The same tradition made him contemporary with Abraham, 'father of the faithful and friend of God', who is said to have migrated with his family from Ur of the Chaldees to Haran, the chief city and commercial capital of Mesopotamia, and thence into Palestine. It is interesting to note that it is precisely with the period of Hammurabi that Hebrew tradition elects to link up its early memories of origins. We might then be naturally drawn to examine the native records of the Hammurabi reign, including its laws, simply to gain a clearer idea of the circumstances among which Abraham was born and grew up. But there are other reasons for our effort to study the period. As a record of early law the Code of Hammurabi is one of the most remarkable monuments of the history of the human race. Treated as a legal document the peculiarities of the Code are amazing. Doubtless an expert in comparative law could have reconstructed a large part of the Babylonian law from the many thousands of legal documents of all periods which have come down to us. To a very remarkable extent this has been done, especially by PROFESSOR KOHLER, assisted or followed by PROFESSOR PEISER, PROFESSOR MEISSNER, PROFESSOR SCHORR, PROFESSOR UNGNAD and a score more who have taken up special points.[13] My article on Babylonian Law in the *Encyclopaedia Britannica* will give some idea of this work.

But while abundant evidence was available as to commercial matters, such as the disposal of estates and other property by sale or exchange, or their assignment by hire, lease, or hypothec, the laws of deposit and warehousing, commenda or commission, agency, security, pledge, warranty, the laws of partnership, rules as to debt and interest, loans with or without security, the family laws relating to marriage, divorce, adoption, inheritance, maintenance, &c., and many other points were made out with great clearness, yet much remained obscure.

For the legal documents, deeds, contracts, or the like, while doubtless absolutely clear to the contemporary parties concerned and evidently the outcome of long-established legal practice, assumed much that could only be conjectured from their slight hints. In my article on Babylonian Law and in *Babylonian and Assyrian Laws, Contracts and Letters* I gathered up most of what was then known.

Especially was our knowledge defective in the matter of criminal law. We had plenty of legal decisions, but they too often merely recorded the award of the court, and even where the case in dispute was stated, the suit was nearly always about property. We had little or no information about such questions as murder, manslaughter, theft, adultery, assault, and the like. The Code, with its full criminal sections, was thus doubly welcome.

The state of society revealed, and its laws, are most remarkable. The tribal system has disappeared. The city states with their local customs are being welded into a unity. There is still local government and district responsibility, but the king's judges are over the local elders, and there is appeal to higher courts, ultimately to the king himself. The family is the unit, with great measure of family solidarity and complete indefeasible right over family estate, devolving its rights to individuals as they form new family units, but retaining rights of reversion amounting to a strict entail.

There is a settled population, engaged in agriculture and pastoral pursuits, yet with many industries in the hands of guilds of artisans, recruited by adoption and apprenticeship, but largely hereditary in families. There is a highly organized system of military service and the *corvée* or press-gang for public works, with a feudal tenure, alongside tenure on payment of tithes and temple dues, and the metayer system by which the landlord found cattle, agricultural implements and seed for culture of the fields. Estates bore permanent responsibilities which went with the land to furnish military service, produce, supplies, &c., to the state. Other estates were held of the king, on rent or tribute, the usual lot of conquered territory. There was a numerous and wealthy body of merchants who were also bankers or moneylenders and much controlled by the Code, especially in the interest of the poorer debtors. They were also afforded state protection and their canvassers carried trade far and wide to every quarter. There was a highly developed and rapid postal or messenger system, of which many beside the king availed themselves.

The land was full of populous towns with fixed areas of dependent villages, remnants of the old city states, now conterminous over the whole kingdom; counties we might call them, parishes and boroughs. There were still traces of borough law, but the Code was supreme and the king's justice ran everywhere. Temples, mansions, farms, plantations, common pasture, feudal estates, existed alongside private ownership in land.

The state of society bears surprising likenesses to that of Europe in the Middle Ages.

The law itself is no less advanced. Justice has replaced vengeance. Self-help is restrained, if not suppressed; wrong must be redressed at law. There is full protection for the weak, the widows and orphans, as the lawgiver himself points out with pride. Women are placed in a position of freedom and independence of their husbands, such as they have only enjoyed in our land since the Married Women's Property Acts. Education was at such a high pitch that

Hammurabi assumes that every injured person would come and read for himself the laws that applied to his own case, or at least find a neighbour who could do so.

The nature of the legislation is no less surprising from a comparative point of view.

In many respects we find the most extraordinary medley of ancient and modern laws. To take but one or two examples. A belief in witchcraft is not avowed, but recognized as demanding regulation ; while purgation of the charge is referred to ordeal by water, such as lingered on so long in Europe.

The extraordinary confidence in the power of the oath to secure truthful witness is remarkable ; but has not died out of our law courts yet. The purgation by oath is in the Saxon form, and applies not only to things solely within the knowledge of the accused, as loss of entrusted goods, but also to manslaughter.

In connexion with feudal tenure we find precisely common-law dower, the right of a tenant in fee-simple or entail to the enjoyment for her life of a third of the undevised lands of her husband which he held in that possession. An attentive examination of the tenure of a Babylonian retainer of the king, who held land on military service, or other royal service including public works, subject to strict entail unless forfeited by failure to carry out commands, will reveal strange likenesses to the feudal system.

The Romans have usually been regarded as inventing the institution of the will, as Sir Henry Maine pointed out, which has played so great a part in modern society, but like the contract, we have it in the Code and contemporary practice in no merely rudimentary form. True that in the Code the only case considered is where the will operates within the family, but other cases seem to occur in practice. We find that a man can assign even land, garden, or house by a sealed and witnessed deed to a favourite child, and if so, when his estate is divided by his children at his death, they cannot claim it as part of the estate to be divided ; the favoured child takes equal share with them in the estate left beside his own special legacy. The husband too could leave property to his wife, and she could devise it as she chose, but only to her children by him ; not to her own family, nor children by a later husband. If a father vowed his daughter to religion, he could, by sealed and witnessed deed, give her specific freedom of testamentary disposition of what she received from her father as a marriage portion on taking her vows. She had a right to a marriage portion any way, which was in lieu of a share of her father's estate. If she took it on marriage it was her portion for life, and was equal

to what a son would take as a son's share at her father's death, but if
she died childless it reverted to her family. On taking a vow, she
would have the same portion as if married, but as she would then die
childless, unless her father gave her power to dispose of it by will, her
brothers or family would resume it.

The importance of status is a well-known characteristic of certain
ancient Codes, and is often commented upon as a feature of special
interest.

The Code recognizes three grades of society by dealing with them
in separate legislation. They are called the *amêlu*, the *mushkênu*,
and the *wardu*. Etymology, analogy with other society, and above
all an attentive consideration of their treatment in the Code have
made their meaning clear. But almost every attempt to translate
these words has failed to convey exactly the true position.

The *amêlu* was evidently a man of the predominant class, the
aristocracy, probably men of the conquering race, Amorites and those
admitted by intermarriage, adoption, or other custom to the same
status. We may compare their position with that of the Normans in
England.

In the Tell-el-Amarna tablets *amêlu* is still used as an official title,
the word is akin to the early Arabic *'ulu, ulai*, and may be rendered
'noble'. In accordance with this usage, in Babylonia, the king or
his minister is often addressed in letters of the First Dynasty Period,
in courteous phrase as the *amêlu sha Marduk uballitsu*, or 'the *amêlu*
to whom may Marduk grant life'. The king was thus regarded as
the First Gentleman of Babylonia. Often *amêlu* has to be rendered
'official'. But even in Hammurabi's time, it was extended like our
words Sir or Esquire to mark every person of position, not otherwise
titled. It was accorded to many professions, even to craftsmen and
artisans; but was as respectful as our Mr. Dean or Mr. Archdeacon,
survivals of Magister or Master. Even in the Code it might denote
'a man' simply, and cover the second grade where the law recognized
no difference of rank or status. When the law says, 'if a man accuse
a man,' it uses *amêlu* for 'man'. Hence we may render *amêlu* by
'gentleman' when he is contrasted with other grades, but 'man'
simply when no reference to grade is contemplated.

When on military service, the *amêlu* was an 'officer', having
under him smaller or greater bands of commoners, slaves, or
tributaries.

He was often a person of wealth, as well as position and birth, but
might be poor, through misfortune, debt, or misconduct. For the
most part he was of the Amorite stock, though so many bear genuine

old Semitic Babylonian names that we may assume that old families of wealth and position from among the conquered had been admitted to the ranks of the *amêlu*, doubtless through intermarriage. The *amêlu* dwelt often in a mansion or palace, literally great house, *êkallu*, the Hebrew *hekal*. Such palaces are mentioned as being built for men who certainly were not kings, nor even princes of royal stock. Hence, we may observe in passing, the slave of the palace (§§ 175–6) is not necessarily 'slave of the king'. The city governor usually had his palace or mansion.

We may conveniently render *amêlu* by 'patrician'; and even without implying all that that term would mean in ancient Rome, we see traces of a close analogy in the way in which foreigners attached themselves to the family of the *amêlu* to obtain privileges of citizenship.

The class which has given most trouble to realize was called the *mushkênu*. PROFESSOR SCHEIL, followed by DARESTE, *Journal des Savans*, rendered the ideographic signs used in the Code, MASH-EN-KAK, by 'noble', not recognizing the Babylonian rendering first pointed out in print by PROFESSOR ZIMMERN [14] as *mushkênu*, but already known to me and underlying my first translations. The word *mushkênu* passed into Hebrew as *miskên*, and later into modern languages—Italian *meschino*, *meschinello*, Portuguese *mesquinho*, French *mesquin*—naturally, with modifications of meaning. Its derivation suggests the meaning of 'suppliant', from *kânu*, 'to bow,' and points to a position of inferiority, if not dependence. It had already been recognized that he was less fined for misdeeds, which evidently suggested the rendering 'noble'. But as it turns out, Hammurabi was more severe in his punishment of the aristocracy than of the poorer or inferior class. On the other hand, while the proud patrician insisted on exact retaliation for his injuries, 'eye for eye', 'tooth for tooth', 'limb for limb', the *mushkênu's* injuries were assessed for pecuniary compensation. He was expected to accept a less primitive award, pointing to a more civilized state. The difference in treatment suggests difference of race. They may well have been the subject race, common people without rights of citizenship. There was a quarter in Sippara, the *mushkênutu*, where this people dwelt apart from the houses, with their gardens and broad streets, occupied by the patricians. This also points in the same direction. We know that the guilds each occupied its own quarter, as in many mediaeval cities, but these had already won, or never lost, the right to rank as *amêlu*.

The *mushkênu* was not necessarily poor, for (§ 15) he had slaves and goods. The earliest copy of the Code sometimes gives *amélu* where the later reads *mushkênu*. MÜLLER had called him an *Armenstiftler*, but there is no trace of his receiving a pension. KOHLER, PEISER, and UNGNAD call him *Ministerial*, but adduce no evidence that he had any special relation to government or clergy. HOMMEL thought him a dependant of the priests, comparing the Hebrew Cohen.

The word, as MR. COMBE has shown in *Babyloniaca*,[15] is found in Arabic—*masâkîn*, used of those who are not *sâdèh* (plural *sayyid*) descendants of the Prophet; nor *mashayikh*, 'nobles', affiliated to the family of the Prophet; nor *gabâyil*, 'secular nobles'; but including the 'labourers', 'workers', 'merchants', 'schoolmasters', 'sycophants', and 'mendicants'. They are unable to carry arms, have no organization, and are entirely under the domination of the nobles. They cannot in any case change their condition. This seems to have been their exact position in ancient Babylonia also, at any rate in somewhat later times.

The *mushkênu* may have descended to a lower position in Babylon, for the phrase, *ana mushkénûti alâku*, meant 'to go to misery', 'to be ruined'. We may even note steps in this degradation. In the Tell-el-Amarna tablets, Amenophis king of Egypt answers the letter of Kadashman-Ellil, the Kassite king of Babylon, who had inquired after his daughter the princess Tsukhartu, one of the Egyptian king's matrimonial alliances. The Babylonian king says that Amenophis had had his sister to wife, but no messenger of his had ever been able to converse with that princess, or to know whether she was alive or dead. They had indeed seen a certain lady, but whether she was the daughter of some *mushkênu* they could not tell. They hardly suspected her of being a poor man's daughter, only of being a 'commoner'. So too, in the days when Babylonia was subject to Assyria, the Babylonians complained that they were being treated as *mushkênu*, not surely as poor men merely, for the obvious answer would be to increase their taxes, but as inferiors subject to indignities.

At any rate, in Hammurabi's Code they are free and possess moderate means, but are inferior persons to the *amélu*, yet superior to the slave.

We see that these poor men fell later into still more abject conditions. In the later texts it is usually their weakness, helplessness, and poverty that is dwelt upon.[16]

Hence my first rendering was 'poor-man', but later I preferred to use 'plebeian', to which view most scholars have now come round.

The slave, *wardu*, was often spoken of as ' a head ', as if he were a chattel, or a mere animal. He was perpetually changing hands, being sold or pledged (§§ 118, 147). Any damage done to him had to be paid for, but the compensation went to his master (§§ 213, 214, 219, 220). If he repudiated his master's rights to his service, he was punished by mutilation. It appears that his master had no power to kill him, but he could brand him and put fetters on him. Yet the slave could acquire wealth and often acted in business as a free man, but his master had control of his actions and took a share of his profits. If he was living in his master's house, he could not buy or sell except by written authority from his master (§ 7). Many slaves, however, married and had homes of their own. The master might act as patron and recover debts for them. Presumably they could not plead in Court, though they were called on to bear witness.

A slave, who married one of his master's slave girls, or for whom, as often was the case, a master bought a slave girl to be wife, was usually provided with a house to live in and often with furniture, such as would not disgrace a freeman's home. Here he lived as a simple poor worker. His master usually respected his rights, fed him and clothed him in return for his service and treated him as a poor subject brother. When the master thus set up a slave for life, with wife, house, and home, he often laid it down that the slave should clothe and feed himself henceforth, and specified the extent of service which he would demand. Clearly such was a very modified slavery. Slaves do not seem to have often been retained living in the house long after they grew up to manhood. On the other hand, slave girls and women were kept in the master's house. A master often made a slave girl mother of his children. But if so, these children were not born to slavery, but if acknowledged became legitimate heirs to the master's estate, and if not, were at least free, and the slave mother was freed when the master died. There is no suggestion that a Babylonian master claimed any rights over the slave wife of his slave, beyond some share in such work as weaving and perhaps a few household duties.

The slave who lived in his own house, if active and industrious, might soon acquire wealth, or he might inherit it from relatives. Hence, he might aspire to marry a free woman. In that case, if he remained a slave, his master took one half his property at death and the other half went to his free wife and her children who also were free. Such a free wife of one who was still a slave might bring her marriage portion, inherit property, &c. In fact she forfeited none of the rights of a free woman by marrying a slave man.   Doubtless, in many cases a master preferred his slave marrying a free woman to having to purchase a slave girl for him.   He had to weigh the reversion of one half his slave's acquired property against the value of a family of born slaves, who of course had to be fed and clothed till they were of value for sale or service.   The humane Babylonians were strongly averse to separating a slave mother from her children and they were usually sold in families.

The slave who did acquire wealth often bought his own freedom. The master had to balance the value to him of the ransom paid against the reversion of his entire property at his death.   In such a case, of course, the master fixed the price he would accept as a ransom.   The slave, however, if married to a slave wife would have to buy her freedom also, and buy each of his slave children if he had any.   The prudent slave, therefore, married a free woman.   The slave who thus acquired freedom, if a foreigner, might return to his own land, or join the ranks of the poor men who were free.   He would thus become a *mushkênu*.   This and similar considerations have led several scholars to translate *mushkênu* by 'freedman'. But a freedman is not necessarily a slave who has bought his freedom, but solely one who has been freed.   The distinction is essential because slaves were often freed for other reasons.

A large number of slaves were freed by adoption into the ranks of the *amêlu*.   A Babylonian father usually portioned off his sons and daughters on their marriage.   The sons, later, at his death, also shared what he had left.   Daughters had no further share.   As long as the father lived, if he fell into poverty or weak health his sons and daughters naturally were supposed to maintain and care for him. But they might agree that he should adopt a new son or daughter, to whom he would leave his residual estate, in return for maintenance and care as long as he lived.   We have spoken of a father, but *mutatis mutandis* a mother could do likewise.   Some scholars think that most of the cases of adoption known to us are examples of a father adopting his natural sons by slave girls.   But the adoption is usually accompanied by a ceremony of purification, symbolizing the emancipation from the taint of slavery.   This would not be necessary in the case of a natural son of a patrician father.   He was free any way at his father's death, even if not acknowledged as heir.   Now in all these cases of adoption of a child to care for one's old age, we can presume that the adoptive parent is childless, as in the frequent cases of adoption by votaries, or else bereft of children by agreement with the grown-up family, who willingly resigned their reversion to the parent's estate in exchange for freedom from the care of their aged parent. In some cases, the adoptive parents, hitherto childless, adopt a child with the proviso that if hereafter they do have begotten children, the present adopted one should rank as eldest son or daughter of the family. Many children were also adopted with the consent of their real parents, who were usually paid. This in some respects was a sale by free parents of their children. They had the right to sell a child to be a slave, but this was a sale to be son or daughter in freedom and was often a wise provision for that child's future on the part of needy parents.

The distinctive character of the slave is that he is fatherless by status. It is usual in legal documents to name the father and often the grandfather of the free contracting parties, the witnesses, judges, scribes, &c. No slave, unless we reckon as such a freeman temporarily reduced to slavery, is ever given as son of So-and-so. In fact, 'the sons of fathers', *mâr banûtu*, such as were the *amêlu* and *mushkênu*, are very clearly men of birth. Their birth, marriage, and death were registered and recorded, so that it was easy to trace family descent for many generations. Enough documents are still preserved to us to compile some family trees for a hundred years or more. But a slave was without family. He was even forbidden in some cases to inquire into his real descent. The family honour was very strictly guarded.

But though occupying so low a grade of society, we have seen that slaves could rise not only to freedom but become adopted into the patrician ranks. This privilege might be forfeited and the slave might be again enslaved without hope of emancipation. There was a mark of the slave which was put upon him by a *gallabu*, the barber and surgeon. Some maintain that this mark was a shaving of the head or forelock in a peculiar way. The slave would thus betray his condition, much as a convict does. But this would be soon outgrown and the slave mark was sometimes an irradicable mark; it is referred to as on the arm, and the surgeon could remove it. So some rather think of a tattooed mark. A barber might be induced by a fraudulent possessor of a slave to remove his old slave mark, but if he could be shown to have done this wittingly he lost his hands. If he could prove his innocence of collusion he was released on oath, but the fraudulent owner was treated as a slave-stealer and put to death. If a slave ran away and was caught, his captor was bound to carry him back to his owner, and was then rewarded by statute with a payment of two shekels (§ 17). If the captor kept him hidden in his own house and did not give him to the town crier he was treated as a slave-stealer and put to death (§ 15). If the slave broke away from his captor, the latter had to swear to his non-complicity in the escape and was then free of blame. The slave was not kept in confinement as a rule; he might freely go about the city, and was usually completely trusted to do errands, but he could not leave the city without his master's consent. If a fugitive slave was captured and would not name his master, he was to be taken to the palace or governor's house and there put to the question, and if possible restored to his owner. If such could not be found, the slave was added to the public slaves, available for the *corvée*. Harbouring a fugitive slave was punished with death. The slave when recovered by his master might be put in chains.

The slave ranks were recruited principally by captives taken in war. But there was regular slave trading. A great many slaves were bought of dealers. After a great battle many prisoners were sold publicly. It is interesting to note that the Code contemplates slave dealers often offering for sale in Babylonia slaves whom they had bought abroad. Such might include slaves captured, stolen, or fled from Babylonia, and even Babylonians themselves. If a Babylonian recognized his lost slave offered for sale the law insisted that the dealer should take just what he had paid for the slave abroad. He had to state this price on oath. On the other hand, a Babylonian captive bought abroad and offered for sale in Babylonia was to be set free. So a slave merchant made no profit on any one who had once been in Babylonia before, scarcely an encouragement to rescue Babylonians by buying them in foreign lands. But the slave dealer was sure of his price for both. For the feudal tenant who had to perform military service, and therefore was most likely to be captured abroad, was to be ransomed whenever possible by his own family, if not by the local treasury, the temple; if that was too impoverished, he would be ransomed by the State (§ 32).

Of course, a very large part of Hammurabi's Code, as may be expected, deals with matters which primarily concerned the state of society in Babylonia in his day. Much of this was quite unlike the state of society for which the Laws of Moses were promulgated. Deeply interesting as such sections are for the early history of human institutions, we must set them aside if we are to confine our investigations within reasonable limits. Suffice it now to repeat the opinion that the Code is one of the most important documents ever recovered to elucidate ancient history. For this contribution to knowledge the histories of Babylonia may be consulted, for its contribution to the study of ancient law the works of PROFESSOR

KOHLER and PROFESSOR SCHORR, and their bibliographies are most valuable.

It is, however, clear that the Code did not aim at legislating for everything that could occur. It says nothing about murder. That was evidently left to be dealt with by well-established custom. Only it interferes to protect the man, who in a quarrel and evidently in danger of his own life should strike a fatal blow. He was allowed to purge himself by oath that he did not mean to kill. Further it passes sentence of death on the wife who procures her husband's death for love of another man.

What the custom was with respect to deliberate premeditated murder we do not yet know. But a late text quotes as an immemorial custom at Babylon that not even a brigand could be put to death there without trial.

The Code is a digest of customary law, a set of confirmed and enacted precedents. It is not properly a Code in the sense of the fully systematized *Code civile* of France or the German *Bürgerliches Gesetzbuch*.

LECTURE II

In my first lecture I tried to set out in brief some of the most striking features of the Babylonian Code of Laws due to the famous king Hammurabi, especially such as were likely to be useful for our comparison with the laws of Israel. We must, however, have a precise idea of the laws of Israel before we can institute a comparison.

Now this is by no means so easy to obtain as one might expect. It is indeed true that the laws of the Hebrew peoples, as set out in the so-called Books of Moses, have been the subject of uninterrupted and intense study by the Jews themselves for many centuries, and that not only for their antiquarian interest but as of supreme importance for religion and morals in the life of to-day. Most of us have heard of the Rabbinic writings, of the Mishna and Gemara, of the Talmud, and may even know the names of some of the famous Rabbis, lawyers, and doctors who have commented upon them. But, I fear, few of us have any clear idea of the stupendous work which they represent. Perhaps the new Jewish Encyclopaedia may give us a better idea. Christian scholars, such as the famous Dr. John Lightfoot, made much use of the treasures of the Jewish writers, but modern scholars appear to have paid small attention to this type of learning.

Nevertheless we are sometimes assured that the discussions of the Jewish Rabbis embody all the most assured results of modern criticism. Certainly they do contain an amount of material for the elucidation of the Mosaic laws which is almost bewildering in extent. When the traditional information and explanation which they furnish are freely taken into account we shall doubtless be in a far better position to understand much that is now very obscure. Certain it is that some scholars who have made a special study of this large traditional body of interpretation, such as D. H. MÜLLER, NATHAN, and PICK, have been willing to admit most striking likenesses between the Rabbinic rules and old Babylonian law. In fact, it seems to be the case that the later Jewish interpretation of the Mosaic law so closely follows Babylonian law that it may be regarded as no less a commentary on that legislation. Our task would soon be at an end if we could be sure that this traditional view was not strongly influenced by the Jewish exile, but really represented what the old Jewish law was intended to be.   For it is practically indistinguishable from the Code of Hammurabi except for the peculiar usages based upon a separate religion and a progressive interpretation in favour of the criminal due to benevolence and humane sentiment.

Very little more need be said than that the Jews, with their wonderful adaptability to the customs of the land of their adoption which has always rendered them the best of citizens, readily assimilated all that was good in Babylonia while preserving also the best things in their own ancient law and jealously guarding whatever was sacred by its religious value.   Such a course was not only sane and sensible ; it affords a proof of the great hold which Hammurabi's Code still had in Babylonia at the time of the Exile and much later ; it sets the seal of approval on its regulations as the judgement of some of the most penetrating intellects the world has seen, and furnishes a brilliant example of a learned but not pedantic attitude which we may do well to imitate.

We shall have reason to refer presently to some of the later Jewish traditions and to appreciate their value.

It is the case that among Christians also the laws of Moses have been studied with deep interest and increasingly careful scholarship. Possibly too little attention has been paid by the modern Christian scholar to ancient tradition.   At any rate, the chief part of the difficulties which we are likely to find in comparing the two legislations arise from the results of the studies pursued by orthodox modern Christian, or at any rate non-Jewish, scholars which have been carried out for the most part without reference to Jewish susceptibilities or Rabbinic interpretations.

Modern scholarship has succeeded in fixing and separating out of the Books of Moses a number of different sources or documents.   In the case of the laws these may be regarded as different codes promulgated at very different dates, or in some cases mere pious wishes for future observance, ultimately worked up into a loosely combined book written in the interest of a party of religious zealots whose prominence later led to the system of thought known to us as Judaism.

We must accept these results, so far as we can get a distinct notion of them, and refer to the separate codes rather than to a single body of laws known as those of Moses.   No one can venture to dispute these decisions on pain of being reckoned reactionary and obscurantist. These scholars hold the seat of authority, and it would be rash presumption to question their ruling.   Nor have I any wish to do this. Yet it may be hoped that they will pardon a sigh of regret on our part that we are now unable to compare the Mosaic law as a whole with the Code of Hammurabi. It would be so much easier for the lecturer, and the indebtedness of Moses to Hammurabi so much more convincing to you. Sadly as many have lamented the tearing of the great law-book of Moses into pieces as rendering it a mere thing of shreds and patches, they may take comfort that its present condition renders it much harder to recognize the characteristic texture of the Babylonish garment.

For now, when one fancies he can discern a surprising likeness between some clause in the Code of Hammurabi and some verse in the Bible, he is wise to keep his surprise to himself until he has procured and studied the latest critical subdivision of the laws of Israel and satisfied himself to which source or sources his verse belongs. Then one has to ransack other authorities to know whether this ruling is one which is widely accepted, and even more important, whether it had been independently reached or was constructed with an eye to the very likeness to Babylonian law which it dreaded to acknowledge.

Consequently we have to be very careful to-day. We cannot use our comparisons, even if they should suggest identity, to restore to more ancient dates the Mosaic items which seem to be most closely in accord with Hammurabi's laws. For here tradition itself imports many difficulties. If we set Moses the lawgiver at his old place in history, just before the entrance of the Israelites into Canaan, and accept the traditional synchronism of Abraham and Amraphel, then if we accept the modern identification of Amraphel with Hammurabi we are landed in this difficulty: the Hammurabi Code is thus as much older than the Mosaic law as Abraham is before Moses. On the authority of Moses himself that means 430 years. Now the Babylonians reckoned 650 years from the death of Hammurabi to the death of Kadashman-Ellil, who was corresponding with Amenophis King of Egypt while that king was still sovereign of Palestine, and therefore before Moses. This is the lowest figure yet suggested based on documentary sources, and gives at least 700 years between the two codes. How can we reconcile the disparity in dates?

The Higher Critics do not mend matters. They would bring down the date of the early Mosaic laws much later, necessitating a period of more than a thousand years between the two codes. It would take hours to argue out the merits of various systems of chronology, and the truth probably is that we have not yet recovered reliable data to fix either Babylonian or Biblical chronology with sufficient accuracy. Babylonian chronology is, however, in much the better state, and late rulings make the death of Hammurabi fall somewhere near 1916 B.C. But how we are to reconcile such a date for Abraham with the Biblical data is a knotty question to which I can contribute no help to solution.

We have here made some assumptions which may be all wrong. I am often asked with much concern whether Hammurabi really is Amraphel. Now that is a question which cannot possibly be answered until much else has been answered first. Hammurabi we know; his life and reign are as well or better known than those of the Saxon kings of England. But who was Amraphel? All we know of him is contained in the fourteenth chapter of Genesis. He is there said to be King of Shinar. If Shinar in that passage means what it clearly means elsewhere, he was a king of Babylonia, or at least of some part of that land for which Shinar is used as a synonym. But even if Shinar does not certainly mean Singara, part of Assyria, it could quite well be a part of the Mesopotamian area with which the early Israelites became acquainted, and so transferred its name to all Babylonia. But Hammurabi is never said to be King of Shinar, nor of any land but Amurru, Akkad, Elam, &c., or Sumer. The latter name means South Babylonia, where Rîm-Sin of Larsa maintained his supremacy in spite of Hammurabi until his thirty-first year. Till then no one could call Hammurabi King of Sumer, and then it is certain he could be no ally with Rîm-Sin. Hammurabi was, however, always King of Babylon. He could hardly have been called King of Shinar by any one who knew anything about his history.

How comes Hammurabi's name to be rendered by Amraphel? We know that his name was variously rendered in cuneiform, being a foreign name to the Babylonian scribes. But they never spell his name as ending in *l*. It has been suggested that one character which denotes *bi* and can also be read *bil* may have misled some Hebrew writer who transcribed the cuneiform account which he found among the archives of some ancient city in Palestine. There is nothing whatever improbable in such ancient cuneiform records being kept. The discovery of the Tell-el-Amarna tablets proves that the kings of Palestine before the Israelite invasion wrote to their neighbours far and near in cuneiform and in the Babylonian language, and also that they spoke a language closely related to Hebrew. But there is no evidence that they misread cuneiform. Let us go on with the assumptions supposed to have restored the credibility of the fourteenth chapter of Genesis. The first point has been that, assuming a cuneiform record to be translated by a Hebrew writer (? Moses) who knew some cuneiform Babylonian, that writer blundered into misreading the name of one of the most celebrated kings of Babylon, with whose history he must have been little acquainted and whose name he found written in a way to which there is no known parallel. Further, he called him King of Shinar. No tenable suggestion has yet been made as to what cuneiform signs he rendered by Shinar. There also he must have found something to which there is no parallel in the native titles of Hammurabi. There is not a single reason in anything said of Amraphel to suggest anything properly said of Hammurabi, except that the names have two out of four letters in common.

But we are told that this identification is supported by the identification of Rîm-Sin of Larsa with Arioch of Ellasar. Rîm-Sin and Arioch have only one letter in common, though Larsa and Ellasar have three. It is a perfect triumph of ingenuity to identify Rîm-Sin and Arioch, and it has been done on various suppositions. But it is also clear that on no supposition was a Hebrew right in reading Rîm-Sin as Arioch, nor has the former name been yet found written in the form which he has been supposed to have so misread. The confirmation of one blunder turns out to be the assumption of another as bad or worse. But the others, Chedorlaomer King of Elam and Tidal king of 'Nations', are also accounted for by a series of misreadings either in cuneiform or out of it into Hebrew or in Hebrew. Grant, then, all that is claimed for this astounding blunder-exegesis. Amraphel was meant for Hammurabi by a man who persistently misread cuneiform. The cuneiform account being reliable history, we can reconstruct what it said about Hammurabi and Rîm-Sin with two somewhat vague allies in Palestine. But what credence are we to give to this Hebrew writer's reading of cuneiform in the case of the name of Abraham? At what period of Hammurabi's reign was an alliance with his life-long enemy Rîm-Sin likely or even possible? When did either make an expedition to the West under the suzerainty of Elam?

But we might consume hours discussing each thread of the web of fancies which some modern scholars have woven over and about the fourteenth chapter of Genesis. There is no mention in Babylonian or Assyrian documents of any one of the persons there named, nor any event recorded similar to those there placed. This fact neither confirms nor contradicts the Hebrew narrative. The doubts thrown on the historicity of the chapter by higher critics were based on arguments which, sound or not, are in no way touched by any cuneiform texts.

So our question must be put differently. It should be: Was the writer of the fourteenth chapter of Genesis of opinion that Abraham was a contemporary of Hammurabi? I am not sure that he ever heard of Hammurabi or knew who he was. The whole story, if reliable, may apply to some other kings than those usually supposed, and this would suit what little we know of chronology much better. It is precisely the identification of Amraphel with Hammurabi which professedly rehabilitates the fourteenth chapter of Genesis, but at the expense of other Biblical statements equally important. It is always well to distinguish the statements of archaeologists and Assyriologists on unrelated subjects from the results of science. No matter how distinguished an Assyriologist may be, his opinion on other matters than Assyriology cannot be laid to the charge of that branch of knowledge. The statements made in the fourteenth chapter of Genesis may yet be shown to be affected by Assyriological research, but most of the recent speculations about them deserve neither the name of Archaeology or Assyriology.

The effect of modern criticism is to make us cautious in another direction. I have hitherto spoken of the Laws of Moses, and I shall continue to do so throughout my lectures. But I trust you will not misunderstand my position. To speak of the Laws of Moses is simply to use the title which was given to them before the rise of modern criticism and by which they are still most widely known. It does not necessarily assume that any one ever existed at all like the Moses described in the Old Testament. Some regard Moses as the name of a mythical hero—a national ideal into whose personification were run all the mythological material which the Hebrew writers deemed appropriate. This need not be the same thing as to deny absolutely the personality of Moses; for another great conqueror of men, Alexander the Great, most assuredly lived, and one clear proof of it, if we had no other, is that his deeds so impressed men that the Arabic historians ascribe to him just as many mythical stories as they know. You have only to read A. JEREMIAS's *Old Testament in the Light of the Ancient East* to see how almost every incident in the life of Moses may be paralleled by some astral *motif* in the mythical story of other ancient heroes or demigods.

But the effect of modern criticism, astral theory, comparative mythology, &c., on the history of Moses leave him much like a lump of sugar in a cup of tea. We know it was there because the tea is sweet, but details as to size or shape are now very unreliable. Nor does Assyriology help us much, for it never mentions or refers to Moses any more than it does to Abraham, or to Israel even until the days of Shalmaneser, 859–825 B.C.

In speaking of the Laws of Moses then, the use of the word Moses is not meant to imply any opinion or to prejudice any question as to the personality or history of the lawgiver or the date of the law. It is used solely as a convenient periphrasis for the current Hebrew lawgiver, just as Hammurabi may be taken as a periphrasis for the Babylonian legislator. That the Babylonian king originated all or even any of the laws enacted in his Code is not asserted. But the historical case of Hammurabi does remove all *a priori* improbability that a Hebrew legislator could draw up a code of laws at a much later date. Further, it should make us beware of arguing anything from the absence of mention in such documents as have come down to us, for, until the excavation of his monuments, no one among modern scholars had guessed his name or surmised his existence.

. This analogy, while it forbids us to deny the existence of Moses, does not show that any or all of the laws ascribed to Moses were in any sense due to him. But that a leader in the position to which tradition assigned Moses could perfectly well promulgate a code of laws as full and complete as the whole Mosaic law, even for a people in the primitive state of society in which Israel is often supposed to have been at the Exodus, is obvious. He had only to avail himself of the knowledge of cuneiform, available at that time both in Canaan and in Egypt, and import copies of the Hammurabi Code from Babylonia if they were not at hand where he then was. He could exercise his judgement as to what would be suitable for his people, add what he chose, and reject what he disliked. That he did this or anything like it is not asserted, but it would be so natural for any one in his position then that we have no excuse for surprise if we should find indications of his having done exactly that.

Still, nothing depends in our comparison of the Laws of Moses with the Code of Hammurabi on our knowledge of the personality or circumstances of Moses. Much would depend on how much of the Laws of Moses we should consider to be his. In a similar way, the use of such terms as the Book of the Covenant, Leviticus, or Deuteronomy, The Priestly Code, and the like, neither implies nor denies the appropriateness of the terms nor any adhesion to any theory of their source or date. They must be regarded as merely names for more or less definite pieces of legislation. That the balance of argument is in favour of assigning to them the extent usually assigned to them by Old Testament critics may be granted for purposes of comparison. It is an opinion which may not be shared by all. But it is not by any means essential to our comparison that any one of the views now held about any of them should be final.

Thus it is enough to grant that the Book of the Covenant is the sole relic of the earliest Hebrew legislation and that the rest may be

regarded as later development.   In that case, however, it is incumbent
on those who hold the theory of this development as an evolution on
native soil to show intelligibly what influenced the particular form
which that development took.   Our comparison may suggest that if
this supposed later law be really not of the Exodus period also, and
not a product of the same mind which modified Babylonian law into
the Book of the Covenant, yet its likeness to Babylonian law excludes
the idea of a free uninfluenced development.   We may hold further
that early or late Babylonian influence is still there.   And we must
account for its persistent influence.   On the supposition of its being
later than the Book of the Covenant we may be inclined to hold that
it was adopted, not directly from Babylonia, but from the relics of
pre-Israelite Babylonian influence on Canaanite law.

It may be asked at once—what do we know of Canaanite law?
Confessedly very little; but so far little attempt has been made to
inquire into the subject.   Scholars have been too ready to endorse
the judgement of the old Jewish writers who denounced all Canaanite
usages.   As yet no documents of Canaanite production have been
found, unless we include those of near neighbours like the Phoenicians,
Moabites, and Northern Syrians.   We may deduce something from
the Old Testament, but that is a hostile source.   A certain amount
of information may be collected from the Tell-el-Amarna tablets,
which supply evidence for times before the Israelites entered Canaan.
Much of the law or custom witnessed to by later times may really be
very old.   Some scholars of late have argued with great force that
the First Dynasty of Babylon were not only Amorites but came into
Babylonia from Canaan.   There were Amorites left in Canaan when
the Israelites settled there.   If these were of the same stock, much
that in the Code of Hammurabi marks change from the old settled
Babylonian Semitic law may be due to a Canaanite source.   The
subject of the Amorite characteristics, apart from their peculiar
proper names, has as yet received next to no attention.   The
researches of Macalister on Palestinian soil will be awaited with
great interest, as he appears to have recognized such distinct
characters about his Amorite finds as to enable him to identify
them as such without hesitation.   He will, it is to be hoped, soon
tell us something of their civilization.   Gradually, no doubt, we shall
be able to tell what was the exact character of each of the peoples in
Canaan; and in the end the Code of Hammurabi may prove to be
the best witness we have to the Canaanite law.

The Laws of Moses were once, and in some quarters still are,
supposed to be all contemporary with that great national hero and

lawgiver, and to form a complete body of law imparted to men by
Divine inspiration. The Jewish commentators, however, of old
treated this view with considerable freedom. Modern scholars, who
have devoted two centuries to a critical study of the Pentateuch, have
lately gravitated towards a fairly definite theory implying the existence
of several codes, so to speak, and those of very different dates, all
much later than the time of Moses. As experience shows there is
very little permanence about the critical views, we had best confine
ourselves to the latest presentation. We need not trouble to inquire
into the merits of the earlier critical theories, and may leave their
refutation to the last writer on the subject. We may take two good
examples for our purpose. Mr. S. A. Cook in his excellent work
The Laws of Moses and the Code of Hammurabi assumed the critical
view of the Pentateuch as then presented, and made the most successful defence of the originality of the Mosaic Law yet attempted. It
will be noted that one of the so-called 'destructive' critics made
a most vigorous defence of the uninfluenced character of the Mosaic
fragments adjudged by that school to be early. Naturally so; for
such critics it is vital to maintain the exclusion of external influence.
There is no criterion of date for them if the orderly continuous
evolution along well-known lines can be supposed to be overwhelmed
by a catastrophic influence from without. The history of the development being unknown or rejected in favour of a theoretical reconstruction upon lines evolved out of the supposed results of comparative
law, religion, or the like, it was delightful and easy to build up a purely
imaginary self-consistent view of the order in which ideas developed
or evolved. The consistence of the view impressed its authors as
proof of reality. There was no history to test the reconstruction
by except such as could be brushed aside as unreliable because incon-
sistent with the view. But some late things, dated as late upon this
theory, turned out to be a thousand years older than the early ones,
and so the almost forgotten maxim 'what is primitive need not be
old' had to be revived. For the evidence of the Hammurabi Code
had to be rebutted anyhow.

It is most remarkable that the champions of the traditional view
never seized upon the Code as a weapon to beat the critics with, while
the Rationalists made a good show of learning and even indulged in
argument on the matter. But after the dust of controversy cleared
off it was perceived that the Code was a new fact to be reckoned
with, neither attacked nor minimized nor exploited, but studied and
respected. As it had surprised and even disconcerted the lawyers, so
it had gradually compelled divines to reconsider.

A work which freely accepts the critical division of the Hebrew laws is PROFESSOR C. F. KENT's book—*Israel's Laws and Legal Precedents* in the *Old Testament Student Series.* If any modification of critical views may have been thought necessary as a result of the new material provided by the Code of Hammurabi, it is here tacitly but fully allowed for. Further study may be expended on the comparison and somewhat modified views may have to be taken, but the nature of the questions involved is clearly and concisely shown in this work.

Were it possible to institute the comparison between the Code of Hammurabi and the whole Hebrew legislation treated as one indivisible body of laws, it would be much less difficult than when a set of regulations are picked out as early and treated as the only rules which deserve to be regarded as in the remotest sense Mosaic, while all else is treated as later and scarcely to be regarded as law at all, but merely pious wishes or aspirations. By such a careful selection there is not only very little to compare, but the very things ruled out as late or unhistorical aspiration on account of their relatively high tone are just those most like the Babylonian. On such principles with criteria so carefully selected to rule out all disagreeing evidence a verdict is easy to attain. It is the fact that these criteria were invented before the Code of Hammurabi was dreamt of, but it does afford a very strong test of them and should lead to some revision. The critical theory is now so firmly rooted in the minds of all scholars who are not allowed in youth to imagine any alternative that we too must accept it or be lost in a perfect morass of unintelligibility. Only we ought to remember that in so doing we make the comparison as difficult and complicated as possible.

Accepting the present division of the Hebrew laws it is possible to divide the periods of Babylonian influence on Israel correspondingly. The conclusion to be drawn is that Babylonian influence was strong in the case of the earliest Israelite law perhaps through common Semitic custom, recalling that Abraham traditionally came from Ur of the Chaldees through Haran, a Babylonian Province, to settle there under strong Babylonian influence where Babylonian language and writing were still used down to the time of the Exodus. The impression of Babylonian is said to be less prominent in later codes until after the Assyrians, whose civilization was specifically of Babylonian origin and type, had held Palestine vassal for two centuries. The Exile was to Babylon itself, and Babylonian influence is naturally strongest after the Return from the Exile, and even more powerful on the Jewish doctors of later days, many of whom continued to live in Babylonia.

Seeing, however, that there is not yet full and final acceptance of critical views as to the exact classification of the Hebrew laws into separate codes, and that my audience is probably not completely familiar with either the separate codes in themselves or their dates, anything like a complete comparison of the Laws of Moses with the Code of Hammurabi is impossible without first at least sketching the character of each separate code. For comparative purposes we may begin with the earliest and see how it compares with Babylonian law, for the rest what has already been compared need not be repeated, but as it is necessary to limit our time I must leave all critical reasons for assigning a passage to a particular stratum to be consulted in PROFESSOR KENT's volume and the extended literature which he names.

The usually accepted critical views of the sources of the Pentateuch regard the Book of the Covenant as the oldest code of Hebrew law now preserved to us. What law the people obeyed before we are not told, but it is obvious that they were not without law. Some scholars, attaching great weight to the traditions of the patriarchs and the implications of their story as to the growth of the people of Israel, assume that before the adoption of the Book of the Covenant they were nomad pastoral folk, and obeyed much the same customs as the Bedawin Arabs of the present day. For such a standpoint the late PROFESSOR W. ROBERTSON SMITH's works on Semitic civilization, religion, and law are simply indispensable. Here, if anywhere, we can find a clear idea of common Semitic custom, so often appealed to to account for the similarities between Jewish law and the Hammurabi Code. But other scholars look on these narratives of the patriarchal life with deep suspicion as being a late attempt to sketch, in the light of a writer's knowledge of what the nomads of his day were like, an instructive and edifying ancestral background for a set of very dissimilar tribes or clans, whom some political necessity led to amalgamate into the Hebrew people. A great deal in our research naturally depends upon our attitude to the questions, 'Was Israel ever in Egypt?' or 'Was only one party of them ever there?'. Or again, 'Was the Book of the Covenant promulgated at the unification of the component clans, or did it grow up long after?' All such and many similar questions we must lay aside, as we start with the Book of the Covenant as accepted Israelite law.

We cannot suppose the Book of the Covenant preserved in its original state. Even if we suppose it was promulgated solely to decide those cases on which conflicting usage was causing disturbance, say between nomad Israelites settling down and the long settled

Canaanite town dwellers; no one can be prepared to claim that it is complete. There must have been more of it. What we have now preserved may have been cut down to present limits for various reasons. It may be that later legislation superseded some of its regulations which later writers would thus think not worth recording. If the Code had been embodied in a document, that source may have become fragmentary in some way by the time the compiler of Exodus rescued it from oblivion. A careful perusal of the laws of Moses as arranged in their strata, by PROFESSOR KENT for example, will show that Hebrew writers had no hesitation in repeating earlier legislation. Hence we cannot argue that no more was preserved solely because it was embodied in later legislation.

Nor can we feel sure that no additions have been made to it. Some clauses seem to be very incongruous in their present context. This phenomenon, however, is not entirely absent from the Code of Hammurabi, which certainly has not been interpolated. But we must start on the Book of the Covenant, as critics have rescued it from its surroundings and set it down for us.

At once an external feature strikes us. In the Book of the Covenant many have discerned a systematic arrangement of the laws in pentads or decads. The Ten Commandments at once occur to one's mind as a parallel. What is the significance of this partiality for five and ten? We are expressly told that the Ten Commandments were on two tables. We should not be surprised had there been seven. Some will think the human equipment of five fingers led to the adoption of five as a convenient method of remembrance. In some such way five or ten may have conveyed the idea of numerical completeness. Unfortunately the division of the laws made by PROFESSOR V. SCHEIL in his *editio princeps* of the Code is both arbitrary and inaccurate. No one has yet ventured to revise the numbering of the sections into which he divided the text of the Code; though several scholars have pointed out the inconsistencies. The lecturer, however, was struck by the fact that a more natural division at once shows an arrangement in *pentads*; and lately PROFESSOR D. G. LYON has worked out this idea, as can be most conveniently followed in the rendering of the Code given by PROFESSOR R. W. ROGERS in his *Cuneiform Parallels to the Old Testament*. Such an attempt will be resented by some as a purely subjective attempt to work up a likeness to the Mosaic laws and disputed accordingly. But the lecturer was led to it in the beginning solely by the fact that SCHEIL's division did not agree with that made by the Babylonian scribes in the fragments of their copies which have survived. These divisions had no

justification on the stela found at Susa, which divides only lines and
even occasionally cuts a word in two. It shows no indication where
a particular law begins or ends. Hence the Babylonian scribes, as
all modern scholars, have had to divide as their common sense dictated.
But the text on the stela was certainly copied from a clay tablet which
may well have shown division-lines between the laws. At any rate, the
divisions adopted by the Babylonian scribes, even if not original, have
great weight as embodying an independent tradition among scholars
who surely knew the meaning and connexion of the successive regulations in a very authoritative way. That their ruling does not agree
with Professor Scheil's where we can compare them shows that his
division is not essential and may be neglected. Unfortunately our
fragments of later copies do not help us often, and are too few to give
us a canon upon which we can rely when we need it most, and we
can rarely be sure that the division we propose was that of the
original. Nevertheless there is great verisimilitude about Professor
Lyon's proposals, and it is a very striking likeness between the Book
of the Covenant and the Code of Hammurabi that both adopted
a division of laws into groups of five. We cannot press the argument
too far, but the Roman Law at any rate shows that this arrangement
is not a logical necessity nor a psychological demand of early
legislation.

The critical account usually given of the Book of the Covenant is
that it embodies the consuetudinary law of the early monarchy. It
is regarded as embracing the formulated decisions which had gradually
accumulated among the people up to that age. It is admitted that it,
or at any rate parts of it, may well be older than the narrative (E.) in
which it was incorporated. Its place in the scale of civilization is
estimated by the fact that it imposes many restrictions on the arbitrary
action of the individual, while it retains the *lex talionis*. Further,
prominence is sometimes given to the fact that God is regarded as
the immediate source of punishment. It is styled theocratic law,
but breaks away from the purest type of such laws. The Code of
Hammurabi goes further in the direction of purely civil enactment.

The picture which W. Robertson Smith draws of the state
of society contemplated by the Book of the Covenant is founded
on the assumption that there was no more of it. The basis of life is
agriculture, cattle and agricultural produce constitute the chief part
of wealth, and the laws of property deal almost exclusively with them.
Only we cannot say that this was all. True, there is no longer preserved any regulation of the relations between principal and agent,
if such ever existed. There is no widely extended tariff of wages for

artificers and workpeople. Too much cannot be made of the fact that the Code of Hammurabi proves the existence of such specialized classes in Babylonia. For it does so without ever mentioning them in just those laws which can best be compared with the Book of the Covenant. If we were acquainted only with that part of the Code of Hammurabi which does correspond to the Book of the Covenant we might similarly construct from it a picture of the state of society in Babylonia just as simple as the Book of the Covenant warrants us in recognizing in Israel. Nevertheless it was not so.

The fact is that the Book of the Covenant does not present a complete picture of the state of society in Israel in the early days of the monarchy. That may not have been so advanced as in the days of Hammurabi. But the kings of Israel at any rate had need of skilled workmen. We read, indeed, that Solomon had to send to Hiram of Tyre for certain workmen, but this is not enough to prove the entire absence from his dominions of other classes of artisans. The absence of blacksmiths in Saul's time is ascribed to an exceptional cause. In fact, the only way in which the entire absence in Israel of all but agriculturalists and shepherds could possibly be accounted for is by supposing that the Israelites had killed out all the Canaanites. We know they did not. We may point out other ways in which it would be dangerous to deduce from the absence of mention in the Book of the Covenant the non-existence of any particular institution whatever.

It is of more importance to notice that the principles of criminal and civil justice are those still current among the Arabs of the desert, namely, retaliation and money compensation. It is precisely the same with the Code of Hammurabi. If these features in the Book of the Covenant compel us to consider the Israelites for whom it was compiled as nomads in much the same state of civilization as the Bedawin, the same features compel us in the case of the Code to ascribe similar civilization to the Babylonians of Hammurabi's period. The fact probably is that in both cases the dominant folk, Amorites or Hebrews, really were conservative of customs once in place in the desert if not too unsuitable for a settled life to retain.

It is a truer way to present the facts to say that both the Book of the Covenant and the Code of Hammurabi do not so much enact the *lex talionis* as interfere to limit its action in certain directions. For example, it is scarcely correct to say in either case that murder was dealt with by the law of revenge or left to the avenger of blood to punish. In the Code murder in general is not mentioned;

we cannot suppose it condoned. But as in the Book of the Covenant it is distinguished from manslaughter, and this is expressly exempted from the death penalty. The innocent man-slayer might take refuge at the altar, as was still the case with those who feared for their lives down to the time of Solomon. It is clear that a murderer might do the same, for he was to be taken thence. Some sort of trial must have taken place before he was delivered up to the avenger of blood. We are nowhere told what was the procedure in Babylonia, but we may assume it was the same, for the innocent man-slayer was liberated on oath of want of malice. The oath was taken at the altar or before the emblem of the god. It is singular enough that no penalty for murder is stated, but there is nothing whatever to indicate that it met with different treatment in Israel and Babylonia.

In both legislations man-stealing is reckoned with murder and punished by death. So is witchcraft, according to the evident implications of the Code and the express declaration of the Book of the Covenant. That offences against parental authority were treated differently is to some extent true. They are summarily dealt with in the Book of the Covenant with a death penalty. The Code spares the son for a first offence in such crimes as would naturally disinherit him, and enacts mutilation for violence to a parent. One may question whether death or loss of the hands was the worse penalty in Babylonia, and may remember that some critics hesitate to ascribe the law enacting the death penalty to the Book of the Covenant. The fierce resentment of the sons of the desert against any form of mutilation would account for the substitution of the death penalty. Other cases of injury in the Book of the Covenant are treated as proper occasions for self-help or for private suits to be adjusted at the sanctuary. That is exactly the view taken by Hammurabi, only explicit provision is made for suits which cannot be so adjusted by judges. Contemporary legal practice bears witness to frequent settlements ' out of court '.

The case of the goring ox is treated by both legislations. Both make no amends to the victim of the attack made by an animal suddenly become savage. Here the Hebrew Code orders the death of the ox, a piece of useless barbaric revenge that has only recently died out amongst us. The poor beast got no trial and could not plead, but was held responsible. This may be very human, but it is to the credit of Hammurabi that he is at least silent on the point. On the other hand, if the ox was known by his owner to be vicious and death resulted, the Code inflicted stated fines on the owner according to the estimated value of the life destroyed. The Book of the Cove-

nant does the same, fixing a ransom for the death of a slave to
be paid to the owner, but death of the ox's owner if the man killed
be a freeman.   And again, the ox is killed.   The difference between
the two fines for the death of a slave is noteworthy as probably
marking average value in each case.   This illustrates the reason
why other fixed money payments do not correspond.   Money values
differed.   Otherwise the treatments could scarcely be more closely
alike.

In the case of specific and particular bodily injuries both laws
exact a retaliation.   The Book of the Covenant is here the more
explicit : ' life for life, eye for eye, tooth for tooth, burning for burning, wound for wound, stripe for stripe' is more detailed at any rate
than the Code, which only enumerated ' eye for eye, limb for limb,
tooth for tooth '.   The difference, such as it is, can hardly be pressed
as really giving a different complexion to the legislation.   On the
whole, despite its extra detail, the Hebrew law is less clear, and the
arrangement certainly looks like a hasty compilation.   For as it stands
these words occur attached to the case of a woman with child hurt by
blows.   At any rate Exodus xxi. 24–5 introduces them with the
words ' and if any mischief follow'.   It may be, as some suggest, that
they have slipped in here from some other context, or be merely
an expansion of the ordinary ' eye for eye ' to give a fuller formula-
tion of the *lex talionis*.   But it is difficult to see how the loss of
a limb, or an eye, or a burning could be the mischief done by a blow
to a pregnant woman.   Miscarriage or death, or both, are the mischiefs
likely to happen.   The Code of Hammurabi deals with the case more
reasonably.   In fact, as it stands, the Exodus passage, xxi. 18–25,
looks very like a loose summary of Hammurabi (§§ 196–200) without
its logical connexion.   At any rate, it is hardly credible that this
collection of words was ever put forward at any time in the world's
history to enunciate a new law for a community of any type that ever
existed.   The most intelligible way of regarding this clause is as an
attempt fully to enunciate the law of retaliation, and that its presence
in its present place is due to the desire to explain some phrase which
less effectively quoted that law; but in the quotation of the fuller
statement the fact was overlooked that some of its clauses were
unsuited to the cases under consideration.   It is no excuse to say
that it looked back over all the preceding cases of assault, for ' burning ' nowhere applies.   The only clause which really applies is the
first, ' life for life '.

Doubtless some critical rearrangement may be made to justify the
use of the clauses somewhere, but as it stands it looks like a stupid

interpolation or an undiscerning quotation of the law of retaliation bringing in the sense ' if any mischief follow then it shall come under the law of retaliation '. That would yield some sense if interpreted with common sense in particular cases. The Code of Hammurabi is much more distinct. If miscarriage followed, a fine was set down. If the woman died also, the assailant's daughter was put to death when the dead woman was of patrician family, otherwise a fine was set down. The Book of the Covenant evidently held to the strict retaliation throughout, but gave no hint as to how it was to be carried out. The Code slips into the same vagueness if the assailant had no daughter to pay the penalty of her father's fault.

In the case of the injured woman in Exodus xxi. 22, the punishment, if no mischief follow, was left to be assessed by her husband, obviously for motives of delicacy; but the decision of the amount to be paid lay finally with the judges. In Hammurabi's Code it was fixed by statute and graded according to the status of the woman (§§ 209–14). What, we may ask, is the essential difference? Can any one suppose that in Israel the husband could demand and secure what compensation he chose? Surely the Hebrew law is a concise way of saying the same thing as Hammurabi's Code does. The scale of payment could hardly be expected to be the same in both lands owing to the difference in money values. A discretionary power in the judges, or a liberty of composition between the parties, is implied in the Code which everywhere states maximum penalties. This is made clear by contemporary practice. Both legislations further take into account the possible death of the woman herself. Else, what is the meaning of the phrase ' and if mischief follow '? The Hebrew law, however, in that case legislates most awkwardly for what could hardly happen in its endeavour exhaustively to express the law of retaliation which was to rule the case.

While we are comparing the laws as to assaults and their penalties, we may pause to note one conspicuous difference between the legislations. The Babylonian lawgiver made a considerable allowance for class distinctions. His was eminently class legislation. Some at once feel that this fact places his law on a lower level than the law of God. Such is a grotesque misapprehension. In Babylonia there was what we have not yet attained nor can do until the State bears all law expenses and gives a poor man justice free of cost. There was one and the same law for both rich and poor. But the aristocrat was treated differently from the commoner. In the eyes of some this is a far worse crime than favouring the rich against the poor, which is the vice of all democracy. But Hammurabi was in this much finer than we might expect, for he treated the aristocrat more severely in every respect than the man of humble birth. I do not attempt to defend that method, but it does need a little explanation.

The facts are these, the aristocrat in Babylonia took a very high view of his personal dignity as one of the conquering race. On his continued support and loyalty the safety of the throne, and consequently the welfare of all Babylonia, depended. The commercial-minded Babylonians, rich or poor, like any other commercial group in the history of the world, could never defend for long even their own money-bags, and for all their industry, brains, and wealth could only pay for protection so long as the pay they were willing to offer exceeded the spoil their mercenaries could wring from them. The aristocrat was actually of a lower civilization, as conquerors were always apt to be, but he held the land by force of arms. Hammurabi was as dependent on his noble Amorites as William the Conqueror was on his Normans. He held them to his allegiance in practically the same feudal manner as did William and his successors hold the Barons.

Now the aristocratic *amêlu* or patrician of Babylonia was very sensitive to a personal injury. He would accept no compensation for a blow as might a commercial plebeian. The exact retaliation ' eye for eye, tooth for tooth, limb for limb ' was his sole satisfaction. The *mushkênu* or commoner had to be content with a money payment. So far for the contemporary public opinion. We say that the proud patrician was conservative of a more primitive type of law, which we find to be that of a nomad Semitic folk, the Bedawin Arabs, still. So far as the Hebrew clung to the same law we discern aristocratic views with a lower type of civilization.

But there is no trace of such class distinctions in the Book of the Covenant. It is not, therefore, a higher type of law. It would be lower if it were purely aristocratic in the sense of love of retaliation. Why, we may ask, were there no social grades in Israel? Possibly because in proportion to the conquered the conquerors were relatively more numerous than in Babylonia. Or possibly the conquered were more thoroughly subdued. Possibly also because the references to class distinctions have since been expurgated from our copies of the legislation.

Now let us take the view that the higher law which accepts compensation for injury in place of strict retaliation emerged later in Israel. Are we to regard this as a natural evolution? Surely not. We are not convinced, surely, that it is a higher law or more inspired. It was probably, as in Babylonia, already the older law of the land before the Israelite invasion, the more civilized law of the more civilized inhabitants of Canaan. Later, according to the critical arrangement of the law codes as preserved to us in the Pentateuch, this more civilized custom is growing, and it has to be forbidden in the interests of conservatism (Leviticus xxiv. 22). At any rate, there, after repeating the law of retaliation, differences of treatment are forbidden. Why should this be done, unless they had been growing? Later still, in Deuteronomy xix. 21, deviations from strict retaliation are again forbidden with the words 'thine eye shall not pity'. Once more, we may ask, if compensation had not been a growing custom among the Israelites, why should this effort be made to strengthen the observance of a lower law? Was it solely because of their reverence for Moses and his law, or was it not because it was all along the Canaanite law and so repugnant to the Jewish lawyers? If so, were not the Canaanites in the same position to the Israelites as the Babylonian *mushkênu* to their Amorite conquerors in the old days of Hammurabi?

The cases in the Book of the Covenant where an injury to a slave is treated are not to be compared to those in the Code of Hammurabi. If a slave is freed (Exodus xxi. 26) for a bad assault on him, it is an assault by his master, for which Hammurabi has no notice. Hammurabi's cases of assault on a slave are by one who is not his master. There is nothing here to show that the law was not exactly the same for both legislations for the same cases. As far as our evidence goes one law treats one case and omits the other, the other law treats the last case and omits the first.

As a matter of fact the Book of the Covenant is here not consistent with itself. A man might beat his servant to death, provided he did not 'die under his hand', and go unpunished, but he might not knock out his eye without having to free him. Obviously, then, if he did knock out his eye, his wisest plan was to so injure him further that he should die. In any case he lost his slave. One can hardly help suspecting that these two clauses belong to different periods. What the Babylonian master could do to his slave without incurring punishment we do not now know. If a slave ran away and was brought back his master could put him in fetters. If the slave repudiated his master's authority he was punished by mutilation. But Hammurabi does not otherwise interfere between master and slave. Probably he, too, counted on the master's regard for his own property.

The case of a slave who married a free wife comes up both in the Code (§ 176) and in Exodus xxi. 3. Hammurabi makes the woman and her children exempt from the master's power. So does Moses, if the man had married before he became a slave.   Of course, if his master gave him a wife, the master retained power over her and the children.   We cannot, however, suppose that if the enslaved Hebrew married a free woman while in servitude that the master claimed to treat her as a slave.   Probably, however, the master had power to forbid such a marriage.   Thus there really was no case likely to arise in Israel to compare with that legislated for in Babylonia, which law regulated all cases except this in Canaan also.   The only new regulation which had come into use is the restriction on the man's term of service.   To meet the case of a man who preferred perpetual servitude in domestic comfort to destitute freedom he was allowed to be ear-marked for the purpose (Exodus xxi. 6).

The Book of the Covenant extends the right of release to females (Exodus xxi. 7) with a proviso.   If her master has used her as a concubine he cannot sell her.   Either he must continue to treat her as a wife or give her freedom.   In the Code of Hammurabi the concubine has the same rights, whether she had been slave or free woman originally, if she has borne children.   If she has not borne children to her master she may still be treated as a slave if a slave before. The contrast between the laws is only apparent.   A Hebrew could not sell his slave whom he had used as concubine, although she were childless, and the Babylonian could.   But, it must be noted that the Nippur copy of the Code, perhaps embodying South Babylonian custom such as Abraham may have learned in Ur, omits the clause allowing the sale of the childless slave-concubine.   As a slave she had to go out in three years, if once a free woman, according to the Code (§ 176), which is the case contemplated by Moses who, however, permits six years' servitude as in the case of male servants (Exodus xxi. 7).   If the slave-girl became betrothed to her master's son she rose to the status of a daughter, which conferred freedom despite her previous status.

The Code of Hammurabi punishes kidnapping of a freeborn man with death (§ 14).   To steal a slave was just common theft, and that also was punished with death (§ 15).   Moses combines the two cases in one (Exodus xxi. 16): ' he that stealeth a man shall surely be put to death.'   The clause which adds ' and selleth him or if he be found in his hand ' constitutes no contrast.   It does not appear very illuminating.   For what purpose any one would steal a man except to sell him as a slave or keep him as such is not easy to see.   But it does recall the insistence of the Code that a man-stealer to be convicted as such must be caught ' with the slave in his hand '(§ 19). In fact the Book of the Covenant seems here to have somewhat awkwardly condensed §§ 14–20 of the Code, attempting to make the law apply to any man, slave or free, without expressly naming the slave. But it does name one case which Hammurabi omitted to notice—when the man-stealer had succeeded in selling his capture. The sale might be difficult to prove, but in a country where scarcely anything was sold without a deed of sale on which the Code insists so clearly no buyer would easily be found. In any case Hammurabi could hardly have meant that a man-stealer was only to be punished if he had not succeeded in passing on his captive. How the Book of the Covenant contemplated proof of sale would be found does not appear. It is to be borne in mind that a man-stealer was only likely to attempt to kidnap a child or a slave. Hammurabi legislates fully for both cases ; Moses apparently attempts to include all cases under one term and condenses the carefully distinguished cases of the Code, and leaves a law which as the Book of the Covenant now preserves its regulations can scarcely be called clear.

In the case of grievous assault the Code demands an oath of lack of malice and payment of the doctor. Moses omits the oath, Exodus xxi. 18 f., and orders payment for loss of time. The injured man seems to have been left to get well as best he could, or the doctor may have been ignored because his practices were connected with idolatry. But the words ' cause him to be thoroughly healed ' surely imply the existence in Israel of some sort of doctor. Anyway, the customary justice underlying both laws is the same. If the injured man dies Hammurabi admits oath of want of malice (§ 207) and fixes the compensation. Here in Exodus xxi. 13 Moses allows the right of asylum. This is a most marked difference, and a whole literature has grown up about the question of asylum and the Cities of Refuge. It is impossible here to work out the question. We must, however, notice that the Book of the Covenant does not specify the usage as to asylum at that period. We can hardly quote the regulations given, say in Numbers xxxv, which are held by critics to be of later date and may embody considerable changes. One of these changes forbids the innocent slayer to leave his asylum until the death of the high priest. That is considered certainly to be of late date. It is associated with a prohibition to take a satisfaction for the deed. If this be also late it marks a growing custom or the recrudescence of an earlier usage. Whenever it held sway the ultimate fate of the innocent man-slayer was the same as in the Code. He had to pay a compensation to the relatives of the slain man.

Now we may consider several alternatives. This custom of asylum or purgation by oath, both implied or prescribed in Israel and Baby-

Ionia, was also associated with compensation to the relatives both in Israel and Babylonia at some time. In Babylonia it was so in the time of Hammurabi and, if not in Israel at the time of the Book of the Covenant, some time later before the prohibition.

In Babylonia the man-slayer would be tried on the capital charge before a court. Whether he had to flee for refuge to the temple to escape the avenger of blood does not appear. But the court was certain to be held there, and the oath was before the altar or emblem of the god. In Israel he had so to flee. He had to be tried on the capital charge there. His oath of purgation implies a trial there. Exodus xxi. 14 implies that a murderer would take refuge there. In neither law are the details given explicitly, but we cannot point out any contradiction; all we can say is that each omits what the other records. We must admit, however, that there may have been real and essential differences here.

Cases of theft show much the same treatment, allowing for adaptation to changed circumstances. The burglar in the Code of Hammurabi was killed on the spot and gibbeted before the breach he had made. In the Book of the Covenant this right to self-help is only allowed if the burglary takes place at night. It may be that the Code also contemplates nocturnal burglary alone, as did the Roman XII Tables. There is, however, no explicit statement on the point. The case of burglary in daylight, however, implies the possibility of calling in assistance. That the death penalty should be inflicted in the Code of Hammurabi for the brigand, for the thief who enters a temple or palace, both public treasuries, to steal, for the stealer at a neighbour's fire, are not to be alleged as contrasts so long as we do not know what the penalties inflicted on such criminals should be. We cannot suppose such crimes unknown in Israel or so rare as not to be dealt with. All we can say is that what we have left of the Book of the Covenant does not notice them.

A very remarkable set of differences strikes our attention when we consider the fines for theft or fraud. In the Code of Hammurabi restitution might be demanded up to thirty-fold in some cases or only double in others. In the Book of the Covenant it ranges from double to five-fold. The treatment is certainly completely independent. Actual reasons for the amount of penalty are given in no single case. We may suggest some, with little confidence, however, in their real influence in antiquity.

That the Code of Hammurabi punishes the aristocrat so sharply may have been due to the uneradicated predatory instinct of his Amorite retainers, or to the arrogance of conquerors who were dis-

posed to hold that the conquered had no rights against them. That
the Book of the Covenant instances only ox and sheep may be due to
the fact that its legislation was meant for a pastoral folk entering
upon a new environment. The peculiar numerical calculations which
brought about the penalty of multiple restitution and decided how
many times may have been founded on some theory as to the significance of numbers which now escapes us.

But one point must be carefully borne in mind. The Code of
Hammurabi states the maximum penalty. Its ' shall ' is not impera-
tive but permissive, it may best be rendered ' may '. A considerable
licence was allowed to judges, and there was always appeal to a higher
court and ultimately to the king.

Damage to crops by animals is explicitly treated both by the Code
and by the Book of the Covenant. Hammurabi (§ 57) separates two
types of damage—one where the crop may recover and even benefit
by the growing corn being fed off and trodden by sheep, the other
where the corn in the ear is irretrievably destroyed. It is not clearly
the case, however, which is treated in Exodus xxii. 5. If not, then
we can allege no contrast; but the LXX and the Samaritan Pentateuch add the case of complete consumption. This might be due to
a later acquisition of knowledge concerning Babylonian or Canaanite
usage, but is so distinct that we cannot fairly insist on conscious
antiquarian interest. The case could hardly be left undecided.

Damage by flooding a neighbour's field, dealt with in the Code,
§§ 53–6, is foreign to Israelite soil, irrigation being rare, but the
same type of law is given for damage by fire in Exodus xxii. 6. This
is not referred to in the Code.

The Code of Hammurabi deals at length with the case of property
claimed as lost from a holder who asserts ownership (§§ 9–13). The
corresponding section of the Book of the Covenant, Exodus xxii. 9,
may be said to condense the whole with extreme brevity thus: In
any case of breach of trust, whether it concern ox or ass or sheep or
clothing, or any kind of lost thing of which one saith ' This is it,
the case of both parties shall come before God ; he whom God shall
condemn shall make double restitution to his neighbour '. This
seems to be the best that PROFESSOR KENT can make of the Hebrew.
Now can any unprejudiced person suppose for a moment that this
clause sets out a new law in an intelligible fashion. Is it not obviously
drawn up in the manner of one who is summarizing a well-known
series of enactments ? To my mind it is very difficult to resist the
impression that it is meant to reduce a rather wide and perhaps not
a very uniform series of judgements to a single formula. That the

law thus sought to be simplified was the Code of Hammurabi does not appear, for the simplification is of a type that destroys almost all likeness. Only this may be said : in both legislations, if any man is found holding property his right to which is challenged by another, the claims of both are to be rehearsed before the judges. So far the resemblance is exact, but while the Code takes each contingency separately, and whoever is proved to have made a false claim is judged to be a would-be thief and as such condemned to death, in the Book of the Covenant the culprit has merely to pay double to the man he has defrauded. This is indeed a marked change, if not improvement. But one would expect progress in five hundred or a thousand years of settled life in Canaan. That so primitive a folk as Israel is usually supposed to have been on entrance into Canaan, or even in the early days of the monarchy, should have a law so advanced would be remarkable enough. But we note that apparently the Book of the Covenant wishes to include breach of trust as well as unlawful detention of property.

Now the law of deposit or trust is dealt with in the Code very clearly and precisely. The depositee is responsible for all loss. Even if the deposited goods are stolen from him he must repay and recover at his own charges from the thief if he can find him. If the depositee wrongly denies or disputes the deposit he pays double. One point only is not decided. The thief has, of course, to be killed when caught. But he may not be caught, and his death in any case will not restore the goods. Now Exodus xxii. 7, dealing with deposit also, does not repeat or resume the surely necessary points treated by the Code, but does take up one of its difficulties. If the thief is caught he, too, pays double. If he cannot be produced, the depositee is brought to the judges to see if he has appropriated the goods. The sequel is not stated, but is usually supplied by supposing it covered by verse 11, which, however, formally applies to a different case, the case of animals entrusted to a shepherd or farmer, which is treated in the Code (§§ 244, 249, 267). There unavoidable accidents are cleared by an oath of innocence, just as in verse 11. But as in Exodus xxii. 13, evidence of the animal being killed by a lion is demanded in the production of the remains ; we can hardly regard this as on all fours with robbery from a granary, for example. In the case of negligence or theft of a deposit both legislations require restitution. There are certainly differences, but no fundamental difference of view. No one can deny that the regulations in the Book of the Covenant might have arisen quite independently, founded on natural experience ; but surely, in that case, the law would have explicitly treated more points. These must have arisen in practice. Why were they not treated?

The answer which seems to meet the case is that the Book of the Covenant assumes just what the Code contains, repeats some of it summarily, adds a fresh case or two, revises the penalties, but, if completely preserved, does all this in a rather crude fashion. We may not have it all, and that must not be forgotten. The Exodus passage as it stands has all the appearance of supplementary legislation, and, if it be as early as is commonly supposed, where are we to look for what it assumes already known?

So far we have instituted a comparison between the Hammurabi Code and the Book of the Covenant without exploiting the subsequent Hebrew legislation. We have seen great likeness mingled with decided contrasts. We have followed quite carefully critical views without being able to exhaust all the ramifications of criticism. We have taken the usual acceptation of the Hebrew laws. Considerations of time and space prevent our extending our researches to the limits of exhausting our subject. Much clearly remains to be done. We could examine most of the points taken up much more closely. Before we leave this part of our subject let us look from another point of view at the cases of slavery already dealt with.

The Book of the Covenant, Exodus xxi, legislates for slaves, both male and female, but especially for those of Hebrew race. A moment's consideration will show that this is not an exhaustive treatment of the questions relating even to them; only selected points are dealt with. Now we may ask, Why should just those points be selected? Was it because the nomads before entering Canaan had no slaves, or were there none of the Hebrew race, or was it the case that in the desert none could sink so low? Or were there no slaves under the early kings of Israel? At what time did the use of slaves arise? Definite ideas on such points are necessary before theories of the date of the laws can be sustained. The usual view is that the institution of slavery is long anterior among the Israelites to the Book of the Covenant, whose regulations introduce no new regulations, only fix customary usages. On the other hand, a very frequent view is that a change in habits on entrance into Canaan had brought new conditions and so had given rise to new sociological problems. Perhaps the conquest of Canaan added largely to the numbers of slaves. The older views on the subject of slavery had to be modified in order to meet new conditions. The Book of the Covenant on this view did introduce new regulations which aimed at teaching a newly settled folk how to treat particular cases. Did the lawgiver, then, treat the subject *de novo*, or merely adopt regulations already in force in Canaanite cities, or did he seek inspiration from the land to which his people's traditions ascribed their origin ?

Now the answer to such a question depends upon what we can find elsewhere in the people's previous experience in the desert, in Canaan, or in dim memories of far-off Babylonian days. That is to say, if these really denoted distinct epochs in their history with distinct civilizations. For if a law on these points already existed, was recalled, or observed in force, which proves to be practically the same as that here adopted, or could be ascertained on inquiry by Hebrew legislators, then the view that they did not attempt to ascertain it, nor recalled it, nor observed it, but independently concocted a fresh law, and in so doing hit upon exactly the same result as they might have ascertained, recalled, or observed, needs only to be stated to refute itself. An appeal to inspiration to explain this kind of miracle is only laughable, and if the best of men professed to so account for any of his actions in ordinary life, we could only doubt his sanity so long as we believed his sincerity.

The Code of Hammurabi had existed for five hundred years or more, and it shows what a settled folk of same racial type under much the same conditions did achieve on the subject. We must, then, show that the Book of the Covenant treats things differently, or that its author could not well be aware of this Code, before we can safely deny that he is indebted to it. Such reasoning has led many scholars to assert roundly that the Hebrew legislation is derived directly from the Babylonian. But for argument's sake let us start by assuming that the regulations in the Book of the Covenant are original and devised solely to meet the circumstances in Canaan at some early period in the Israelite predominance there, and let us consider these regulations more closely.

The regulations appear to concern a Hebrew slave. The first question we ask in astonishment is : How came a Hebrew to be a slave ? We probably all know of amazing feats of exegetical dexterity achieved over this question. The Book of the Covenant, however, only adduces the one case of a man sold by the judicial authority for a theft which he was unable to restore (Exodus xxii. 3). The later law in Deuteronomy xv. 12 appears to add the slave acquired by purchase. Who had then the right to sell him ? If a Babylonian was captured by the enemy and offered for sale as a slave to his compatriots he had to be ransomed by his own family, his city, or the state, and was restored to freedom and not enslaved any longer. Surely a Hebrew would not be worse treated. The law of P. explains the case more clearly (Leviticus xxv. 39) : ' If thy brother be waxen poor with thee, and sell himself unto thee.' We may regard this as later, but can we deny that the case itself was not supposed all along? It is most probable that the only way in which a Hebrew could become a slave in his own land to serve a Hebrew master was in some such fashion, which is not really slavery at all.

There is no evidence to show that captives in war, reduced to slavery, or the slaves bought in the open slave market, foreigners in either case, would be freed from slavery at any time, under this law or any other. Later, Leviticus xxv. 44–6 expressly sanctions such being ' bondmen for ever', and this was everywhere the natural custom.

The Hebrew ' slave', as he has hitherto been called, contemplated in this law, as understood somewhat later, is simply one who had assigned himself or had been assigned by lawful authority to his holder to work off a debt which he himself had contracted. Such in Rome became a real slave, and might easily have so become in Israel and Babylonia but for Moses and Hammurabi. There is no evidence that a Hebrew was ever a slave in any other sense. We shall return to the point again. This is not really a slave but a hostage for debt. Hammurabi had a special name for him, as had the Roman law. The Hebrew term covers such, using a word that may mean a servant, a hostage for debt, or a proper slave.

This ' slave', then, worked off his debt by unpaid service. When Leviticus xxv. 40 lays down the rule that he shall not serve as a bond-servant but shall be as a hired servant, it bears in mind that he was not a slave at all, but had temporarily lost his freedom. He was like the sojourner, still free, but not fully free. It could not be meant to order that wages were to be paid, only that no such exacting service should be required as was evidently the rule for bondservants or real slaves. ' Thou shalt not rule over him with rigour' is a good gloss on the case. For it was naturally a temptation to the holder to get as much work out of this ' slave' as he could, in order to recoup the debt or purchase-money in view of the approaching release.

It is most important here to note that the law takes no account of the amount of debt. A purely commercial spirit would have estimated the yearly average value of the slave's work above his keep and clothing, and then would fix the term of service at such a length as would suffice to work off the debt and its interest. That such calculations were made in Babylonia is evident from existing documents. In the existing state of legislation in Israel we may assume that a man who was in debt, knowing that if he sold himself for debt he would have to serve six years, would not sell himself unless he saw some fair equivalence between the work he would have to perform in that time and the amount he owed. He could hire himself out as a hired servant and pay off the debt with the money, possibly in less time. So it was ruled that if he did elect to serve out his debt he is not to be made to work harder than a hired servant would have to do.

In the Book of the Covenant, then, it seems that a Hebrew was only likely to get into such a position as a result of crime for which he could not pay the fine or a theft which he could not restore, and so by judicial sentence or by voluntary self-assignment for debt.

In such cases the law rules that whatever was the amount of debt six years' service must be held to discharge it. That opened the way to abuses in two directions. The service might be an insufficient discharge, and so the holder, if the debt was due to him, or the purchaser of the convict, would be cheated; or the man who had suffered the theft be not remunerated. So it is not to be supposed that when a man was sold to pay for a theft which he had committed the buyer would pay more for him than he could reasonably expect to get back by six years' service. Thus the way was opened to a second abuse, excessive exaction of labour from the slave. Later legislation recognized the existence of just these abuses and attempted redress.

Now all this is completely like the Code of Hammurabi, which already provided for the abuses as well (§ 117 ff.). The Code deals with the man assigned, literally 'named', *nibutum*, like the Roman *nuncupatus*, to work off a debt. The Code expressly reserves the right of 'naming' this hostage to the debtor himself. The creditor had no power to seize the debtor or distrain on his goods or dependants. If he does he is fined and voids his debt at once. It also, like the Book of the Covenant, contains cases where a man might be sold with his family, and of course his goods, to pay a liability which he had incurred through culpable negligence. Neither it nor the Book of the Covenant expressly brings this case under the law of release. It does not record the case of a man actually 'naming' himself as *mancipium*. But that surely is not excluded from possibility, and we know from actually recorded cases that it occurred.

The points of difference are (i) the term of service—fixed by the Code at three years, by the Book of the Covenant at six years; (ii) the regulations against the ill-treatment of the hostage; (iii) the regulation for the case of the man who wished to remain a slave for ever.

On these we may remark, first that in Israel the term of six years imposed by the Book of the Covenant was evidently resented, and has to be explained as really a double term (Deuteronomy xv. 18). Surely that indicates a knowledge on the part of the later lawgiver of what was not generally known in Israel, to wit, that the term had once been three years. Where and when, we may well ask? Surely not in Israel, or the creditor would not have so resented a regulation which gave him twice as much for his money. Nor in his neighbour cities of Canaan, or he would still have recognized his improved position. It must have been somewhere at a time now forgotten in a state of things which he would be expected still to respect. Where else could it be than in Babylonia, the home of his father Abraham? Would any one have quoted him a law unless it was one he was likely to respect as eminently just? He may not have known that law by the name of the Code of Hammurabi, but simply as 'ancient law' so highly revered by Orientals in all ages. 'Ye have heard that it was said by them of old time' was enough.

Here some one may be disposed to raise the objection that the creditor was not told that the six years was double the term allowed by ancient law, but simply that it was 'the double of the hire of a hired servant'. Now if that does not mean the same thing it has no sense at all. For a term cannot be double the hire of anything. It is the value in work of the term of service which is double a hire. We must express both terms in the same denomination. In what sense could six years ever be double of anything but three years? How can we imagine three years to have any special connexion with the term of a hired servant? Is there any evidence that servants were usually hired for three years? The term in Israel, as in Babylon, must always have been matter of free contract. The writer has in his mind the other regulation that the hostage for debt must not be treated worse than a hired servant, and explains the six years' term as double what the debtor would be likely to agree to if he was in the position of a hired servant and free to contract about the term. Why should he be thus expected to fix upon three years as a term? Probably because the custom, which had come down from the time when Canaan observed the same usages which Hammurabi codified, regarded three years as a proper term. If this view be thought not convincing, it may be rejected.

It is at least curious that the excuse given for demanding release for a hostage for debt at the end of six years is that this is after all double something—when it actually is double the term Hammurabi fixed. In whatever way the Deuteronomist meant his reader to understand his explanation it is difficult to imagine what else was in his mind. The something which he appears to allege may be a gloss on his words. The text may once have said 'for the double he hath served thee', and a dull glossator may have sought within his own consciousness for the rather pointless example suggested by the other reference to a hired servant's service.

Anyway, the term is explained as a double one, and it was double of the term in the Hammurabi Code.

The second point of difference has a suggestion of greater ruthlessness in Babylonia in treatment of a hostage. 'Blows and starvation' point to efforts to get more out of the hostage. This, too, is the underlying thought of the later legislation in Israel which forbids his treatment as a bondservant.

The third point, too, suggests that in Babylonia it rarely occurred to a man to prefer comfort with servitude to freedom and destitution. The lot of the free destitute may have been more hopeless in Israel, the lot of the slave less tolerable in Babylonia. Or the love of freedom may have been greater in Babylonia. In any case, such a difference in law is the sort of addition which might be expected to grow up in five hundred years of advance, in a different state of society and a far-off land.

In the last resource the ground principle remains the same. A debtor may name himself, or one of his family, or his slave, as hostage for debt, but whatever the amount of debt, the hostage shall not be held beyond a fixed term. This in both laws only applies to a free individual and never affected a real 'slave'.

We have hitherto assumed that the law contemplates only the Hebrew male 'slave'. But are we to suppose that when an Israelite got into debt or was sold to pay an obligation that he alone was responsible? Could not he also assign his wife or child or slave to work off his debt? And if he did, are we to understand that they could be kept for ever in bondage? The words of the Book of the Covenant do not expressly answer any of these questions, but only a very pedantic interpretation of the letter of the law could confine its operation to the male head of the family.

We do have, however, an indirect answer in the next two clauses. He might come in alone or he might bring in his wife (and family presumably) with him. If so, they had to be released with him. The case where he assigned them in his place is not mentioned. Are we to assume that this was not done? Subsequent legislation extended the law. Deuteronomy xv. 17 has 'so shalt thou do to thy female slave'. This may have been necessary to prevent an abuse of refusing to release a female ' slave ' sold to work off a debt, on the plea that she was not covered by the words of the Act. This would be to assume a litigious spirit, of which we have no other proof to allege. It is better to regard it as commentary. It may, indeed, be contended that the law was intended to cover only one special case, but it is more reasonable to suppose that it takes a special case as norm for all.

Now what is this the law of ? To call it the rights of the Hebrew slave is surely to miss the whole point. It is still more misleading to call it the law of male slaves. It is the law of the hostage for debt. It concerns only the person assigned as *mancipium*. No other comes into view. And such is not a slave at all. There is, therefore, here no information about the treatment of slaves in Israel. All the fine talk about the humane character of the Mosaic law may apply else-where, not here. The law simply insists on the release of a debtor held to work off a debt at the end of a fixed term.

The further details of the case in the Book of the Covenant are considerations of special cases—(i) if the debtor is a single man when he enters on his term of service, (ii) or accompanied by his wife (and family ?), (iii) if provided by his creditor with a wife during his service, (iv) if he prefers servitude in domestic freedom to destitute freedom. On these grounds we may remark—

(i) That he should go forth alone if he came in alone merely heightens the contrast. No restraint of the holder's freedom is intended, but a limitation of the debtor's claim. If his holder finds him a wife, and so children, he cannot claim to take them with him, that is all.

(ii) If his wife accompanied him she has the same rights to release as he has. His family is not named, but was surely in the same position. What is here ruled is simply that this class of servitude does not forfeit freedom for any one.

(iii) It is obvious that the holder might give him a slave-woman to be his wife. Had he been fully free the children of such a marriage would be at his own disposal. Now they are the holder's property. As a single man held to work off his debt he probably was not free to choose his own wife. His children were a species of profit to his holder, just as if he were an ox.

(iv) The case where the man chooses to stay is instructive from many points : for a Hebrew could thus become a slave for ever. There were no degradations if no grades were recognized, and there were no religious disabilities. It did not even preclude wealth. The boring of his ear by the awl was a significant way of nailing his obedience, of which the ear was the organ and symbol, to a particular house.

So far in our comparison of the Code and the Book of the Covenant we have been content to show likenesses and contrasts. But there are not lacking cases in which some have not failed to see deliberate conscious change. One of the most surprising things in the Book of the Covenant, if it belongs there at all, is the prohibition to 'favour the poor man', Exod. xxiii. 3. The direction must be addressed to persons in the position of judges. It is sometimes maintained that the Book of the Covenant shows no trace of judges. However that may be, the directions must be addressed to those who decided causes, judges under some other name.

Now why was the poor man not to be favoured? We should not be at all surprised at judges being told not to favour the rich man. It can never have been superfluous in the East. But the Code does favour the *mushkênu*. We have seen that he was called 'a poor man' by several translators after the rendering 'noble' had been given up. That was partly because the Hebrew *meskîn* has always been taken to mean a poor man. Perhaps the original text of Exod. xxiii. 3 had *meskîn*. Then the later redactor, who seems to have known the Code, may have wished to obliterate a tell-tale word. The Code did favour the *mushkênu* in the sense that he could do wrong at less expense than his superiors. Also his offerings in the Temple were allowed to be smaller. Now this is exactly how Leviticus does favour a poor man, and that again suggests that by 'poor man' the Hebrew legislator did mean the same as the Babylonian *mushkênu*. Now if this otherwise very odd remark in Exod. xxiii. 3 was really old, one wonders that the Leviticus law does so favour 'the poor'. But Exod. xxiii. 3 might well be passed later to abrogate this Babylonian tendency. Exod. xxx. 15 expressly forbids the rich to pay more or the poor less. The same word for 'poor' occurs in all cases. Did then the early Hebrew law aim at reversing the Code's rule that 'poor men', or rather 'plebeians', should pay less? We may suppose that the Canaanites were the *mushkênu* in Israel. The 'sojourners' obviously were. But Hammurabi had neither riches nor poverty in view when he favoured the *mushkênu*. By the Tell-el-Amarna period the name had lost its exact value and become even in Babylonia more contemptuous. Later in Israel it became a name for a beggar. Did the Hebrew legislator catch the word when it only conveyed the meaning 'poor', and use his own term to avoid ambiguity?

The idea of God as the ultimate source of punishment is inferred as characteristic in the Book of the Covenant from Exod. xxi. 6; xxii. 8, 9, where the offender is brought 'unto the judges'. These words are now more usually rendered 'before God', as there is no apparent reason why the word usually rendered 'God' should here be rendered 'judges', beyond a late opinion that such was the meaning of the phrase. This opinion is correct in so far as that analogy with Babylonia leads us to suppose that in every trial before judges the parties and the witnesses were put on oath before God. This direct appeal to God as the all-seeing Judge of men is in complete accord with the Babylonian practice, as revealed by the Code of Hammurabi. The conscience of the criminal and the fear of God's vengeance on the perjured were in old times very powerful motives.

It is often said that the Jewish law is theocratic. So it is, when regarded as a whole and in the sense noted in the last paragraph. But this is not the attitude of the Judgements contained in the Book of the Covenant. At any rate they are not more theocratic than the Code of Hammurabi, which is extraordinarily free of religious motive. The type of a theocratic code is the Laws of Manu, a much more primitive type than the Laws of Moses. In some respects the Code of Hammurabi is practically a civil code, and so ahead of the Laws of Moses. But it must not be taken as a criterion of age that the Mosaic law is theocratic, nor pressed as a mark of primitive law. For it is theocratic mostly in a peculiar sense. The civil law of Israel comes to us embedded in a mass of religious law, and prefaced by a narrative of its production, serving to connect it with its divine author. Some portion of this framework bears a strong formal likeness to the Code of Hammurabi. This has been pointed out by S. A. Cook who, however, does not regard it as a sign of dependence.

We must, however, allow some weight, one way or another, to this likeness. Either this setting is original, or it is not. If it essentially belongs to the Book of the Covenant, that is theocratic to about the same extent as the Code of Hammurabi, and another striking similarity is added to the list of arguments for dependence. If it is not original, then the Book of the Covenant, unlike the rest of the Hebrew law, was originally purely civil unless it had a different religious setting (Babylonian or Canaanite?), and so still more like the body of the Code of Hammurabi.

We have two pictures, so to speak, with very similar art and very similar frames. In one case we know the picture and its frame are contemporary. In the case of the other, which is certainly later, both picture and frame are very like the older. If now the later frame be not contemporary with its picture, we cannot use it to conclude that the pictures are independent studies of the same subject. It gives no evidence as to its picture. If the later frame be original and contemporary, the later cannot be treated as an example of art repeating itself. The copied frame is a very significant argument in favour of the later picture being regarded as a copy too. Now it is very important to much of the critical argument that the frame is original.

LECTURE III

In the first and second lectures we have dwelt upon the external features of the two codes of law to be compared, and pointed out some things remarkably similar. We have now to consider the various theories which have been propounded to account for them. The progress of the discussion has shown that the higher critics are as eager as the orthodox Jewish or Christian writers to repel the oft-repeated assertions of dependence.

There are obviously many ways of treating the resemblances and accounting for the differences, and some of them may, and probably will, long be held which do not attempt to take account of more than a selection of the facts. That theory will surely be finally accepted which takes account of all the facts. Hasty dogmatism only succeeds in imposing on the credulous public and provokes the resentment of those whose judgement is alone worth considering. I should esteem it then a real misfortune if anything I might say should lead any one to form a conclusion based solely on what he considers to be my opinion. Therefore I expressly warn you that I have not given you my opinion, nor do I intend to do so. I desire solely to make you aware of the facts, and invite you to form your own opinion.

Now the first thing to deal with is the general similarity of the Code to the Book of the Covenant, considered as our best witness to the primitive Hebrew law. It has been calculated that out of forty-five, or possibly fifty-five judgements preserved in this old Hebrew law, thirty-five have points of contact with the Hammurabi Code, and quite half are parallel. Of course, there are also marked differences to be accounted for. The Hebrew law appears to have legislated for a small people, among whom human life was precious and property scanty. The Babylonian law protects property with far severer penalty, and makes little account of a criminal's life. This is appropriate to a nation of commercial instincts and a wealthy populous state. It recognizes grades of wealth and position. The theft of an ox is punished by a five-fold restoration in the Hebrew law, in the Babylonian by thirty times its value, or in the plebeian's case by a ten-fold penalty. We may estimate the difference by saying that in the desert five oxen was about all a man had, and his

E

family would probably have to help him to pay, and so the penalty was an effective restraint; while in Babylonia, thirty oxen were to many men not more costly, and even the commoner was twice as wealthy as an Israelite.   It is, however, more likely that the penalties were not calculated at all upon an estimate of what they meant to the criminal, but on an artificial system of the value of numbers. For example, in Israel, five may have been ideally complete. PROFESSOR D. H. MÜLLER has most ingeniously worked out the possible significance of the numbers.

It is not particularly profitable to insist upon the superior humanity of either code.   Impartial judges, acquainted with ancient codes, will perceive that the balance between the rights of the individual and those of the State is always very difficult to hold level.   Severe penalties may be due to the determination to suppress crime at any cost.   The desire to save the criminal from the results of his crime is not to be expected of any early legislator.   Only when his life was worth more to the State than the loss he was likely to cause could the criminal hope for pardon.   As Hammurabi put it, the king might wish to save his servant's life.

Points of close agreement are numerous.   The treatment of sorcery, the law of deposit, the punishment of kidnapping, injury to a pregnant woman, regulations as to shepherds, and a score more may be noted as very similar.   These are given in many books, very conveniently in PROFESSOR S. R. DRIVER's *Genesis* in the *Cambridge Bible for Schools*.

Now on such a view of the general similarities many have expressed the opinion that the Hebrew laws are a more or less revised adaptation of the Babylonian law, perhaps as locally already modified in Canaan to suit the prejudices of the invaders while they were changing their habits of life and became a settled people.   But this view is not vivid enough for others.   There is a certain delight which some feel in propounding views calculated to shock some one.   The cruder view that the Hebrew lawgiver, call him Moses or some higher critical periphrasis for the same thing, sat down with a cuneiform copy of the Code before him and copied out the Babylonian laws with some adaptations, may have been enunciated with some such amiable wish, but was too crude to disturb any one.   It is barely worth record. The differences between the Codes are too important for us to adopt it.   If he made a copy it was a very bad copy.   Some allowance for the difference in age must also be made.   Such a length of time as five hundred to a thousand years must have been marked by great changes in Babylonia or in Canaan.   The advent of the Israelites

must have introduced new forces into the life of Palestine. Here
we have to weigh carefully our evidence, which points on the whole
to the Israelite contribution being more primitive in type, and in
some degree a return to early conditions which held before the
time of Hammurabi in Babylonia. Dear as these changes were
to the later Jewish mind, they were not what we should call
improvements.

But when merely considering such general resemblances, along
with such marked differences, we can readily see that a theory of
common origin will suffice to account for the likenesses; while
many subordinate theories can be put forward to account for the
differences. Between the theories of these differences it must be
impossible to decide until we know more accurately the exact
circumstances of the Israelites at, or soon after, their conquest of
Canaan. We may, for example, have to regard the conquest as
extending over a long period and admitting of many gradations of
supremacy in different parts. It is not likely that a clean sweep was
made of the old inhabitants and their customs at any one epoch or
place. We may have to extend this period of conquest down to
the end of the time of the Judges. Parallels are not wanting in the
history of Babylonia. The so-called Amorites had been some centuries
in the land before Hammurabi's supremacy, even before they appear
as founding a dynasty.

A favourite theory of the resemblances is that they are due to a
common Semitic origin. Let us examine that theory more closely.
In support of it we have to show that the common features are of
a Semitic type. This is more difficult than is generally supposed.
When practically the only pastoral nomads whose customs were at
all well known to theologians were the Arabs and, as usually
assumed, the Israelites, many features were put down as Semitic
which are now recognized as rather due to the exigencies of the
nomadic life. The recognition of the Babylonians as a type of
settled Semites led by slow gradations to the admission of other
features as also Semitic, while some things hitherto only known
among Semites have been recognized as the common possession
of many unrelated folk. Gradually, and probably unconsciously,
'common Semitic origin' has become a mere euphemism for
'Babylonian'. For to what part of the Semitic world can we look
for so advanced a civilization as to be common both to the Babylonian and Israelite law? It must be at least as advanced as the
things common to those laws and yet not presuppose a state of
society which could not be true of a Semitic people. It would be

interesting if we can find anywhere a clear sketch of what conceivable state of society the common Semitic origin really implies.
It might then be argued that no such society ever existed. At
present all we can say is that we do not know where to find it. It is
really only a convenient term, like evolution, to conceal our ignorance
of history.

If it could be shown that just those features which are common
to the Hammurabi Code and the Israelite, and therefore presumably
existed in the common Semitic origin, are unlike anything in the
Sumerian or pre-Semitic laws of Babylonia, then the fact of a common
Semitic origin might have to be admitted without our being able to fix
upon a locality for it. In Babylonia a predominance of Semites, at
least in the north, may be dated, perhaps a thousand years before
Hammurabi, under Sargon of Akkad. But while we know of
Sumerian Family Laws and have references to legal reforms under
the Sumerian Kings of Babylonia even in pre-Sargonic times, we
have not yet sufficient material from those early days to know exactly
how far Hammurabi's Code was really an advance upon older
Sumerian law. Slowly but surely we are learning that precisely the
same legal forms were in use, long before Hammurabi, among the
Sumerians of the south. The legal documents of Hammurabi's age
are full of the old Sumerian words and phrases, used just as dog-Latin
or Norman-French was in our deeds of early English times. We
could not claim a common use of Teutonic translations of Roman
law terms in England and Germany, if such existed, as proof of a
common Teutonic origin for the laws. But the Hammurabi Code
is full of Semitic translations of Sumerian terms. This would be
quite fatal to the theory of common Semitic origin but for the fact
that the Sumerians had been conquered so long before by Sargon,
and we cannot yet clearly sift out what may have been due to his
Semitic followers from what may have been imposed on them by the
subject Sumerians. The conquest of Babylonia by Elam may have
affected its laws more than we think. The barbarous Elamite punishments survived in Babylonia, in Mesopotamia, even in Israel, two
thousand years or more. But one can hardly argue much from that.
The early history of Babylonian law is still very obscure, and we can
only state probabilities of more or less cogency.

The Semitic origin seems afflicted by lack of cogency. One
must respect it for the attachment which certain estimable divines
show to it. One rather wonders whether Noah was a Semite as well
as his eldest son, and whether these laws really go back as early as
Shem. Elam had claims to be a Semite, and an early Semitic

kingdom in Elam seems to have been long predominant there. Was Elam the real common Semitic home both of Amorites and Israelites? There was a district not far from the border of Elam over which Kudur-Mabuk, the father of Rîm-Sin, once ruled, and which was known as the land of the Amorites. Thence the First Dynasty of Babylon may have come. Whether the ancestors of Abraham in Ur of the Chaldees were once Amorites or earlier Elamites we cannot yet decide. But with all these speculations scientific folk show small patience: for they have another way of solving the problem.

It is most probable that some of the features which Hammurabi's Code has in common with the early Hebrew legislation are only slightly modified from the still earlier codes which date from the time of earlier Sumerian supremacy in Babylonia. Hence we should remember that a common Semitic origin may really be only a step towards a reference of both to an early Babylonian origin. At present we are not likely to find evidences of early Semitic custom anywhere so early by some thousand years as in Babylonia; and though we are quite justified in supposing that Arab customs may be older still, as they certainly are more primitive, we can never date them with certainty except when we can show them to arise purely and simply out of local circumstances. Then we may perhaps affirm that they must always have been the custom in Arabia and treat them as a witness to early Semitic law. On this side of the question Mr. S. A. COOK's work is invaluable.

But the evolutionist or scientific man has a much easier solution. He has made a comparison of laws among such foreign folk as are wholly unconnected with Semites or Sumerians. It is found that all men everywhere do hit upon much the same solution of the same social problem. We may say that the likenesses we perceive between the Code of Hammurabi and the Hebrew laws are due to the natural dictates of human experience. If we take up the laws, one by one, which are common to the two systems, we can account for almost all the likenesses in this way. Some very remarkable similarities have been shown by PROFESSOR D. H. MÜLLER to exist between the Code of Hammurabi and the Twelve Tables of the Roman Law. PROFESSOR COHN, of Zürich, has pointed out strong likenesses to the laws of the West Goths. On the other hand, DR. H. GRIMME has pointed out some very close agreements between the Mosaic Laws and an ancient Semitic Law of Bogos, which goes back before the coming of the Amhara into Abyssinia. There are some likenesses even with the old Indian laws of Manu, and even the laws of the

Aztecs have been compared. We could not expect much assent if we argued for a common parentage of these widely scattered laws and their descent from the Code of Hammurabi.

The scientific view is that the common laws are due to common human experience, which is much the same everywhere. It is closely allied with the doctrine of evolution as applied to human institutions. If we could only assume that the nations developed each separately and independently, without mutual intercourse, it might suffice. But for ages before the institutions we are considering, both Babylonia and Palestine had been the meeting-place of many peoples. We cannot tell by any *a priori* method which race introduced which custom. All we know is that an improvement is often readily adopted by people from those with whom they come in contact, even when not forced upon them by conquest. But we also know that even superior usefulness or comfort is not always sufficient to keep a custom alive. We now know that without much apparent reason even an essential craft may die out. In fact, this common humanity origin of common customs is very useful, like the theory of evolution, to account for observed results when we have no knowledge of what preceded them and can only guess at the previous history. One can then, without fear of contradiction, assert what we consider most likely to have led up to them as their antecedents. But these easy explanations do not absolve us from careful research where history can be produced to work upon. The evolution of human institutions, if such be a legitimate expression to use, has many a set-back or reaction, and we may very well at any time be comparing progress in one history with reaction in another.

But while the evolutionary theory of human institutions may be appealed to for satisfying our curiosity when no possible answer can be given by history, there are things often to be observed which it does not well account for, and then recourse to it is the reverse of scientific. An illustration taken from the arts may help to clear our minds on this point. It may be assumed that all men everywhere may be expected to hit upon the device of burning clay vessels until they obtain some rude form of pottery and then develop the potter's art to some extent. We may call this evolution. Not only can the making of pots and pans be adduced from all parts of the globe, but truly astonishing resemblances can be discovered between pottery from districts so remote that we cannot believe there can ever have been communication between them. Here an independent evolution has produced the same results in unconnected areas. If that were all, the modern science of pottery evidence would be impossible.

We cannot afford time or space even to sketch here the chief results of the intensive comparative study of pottery, which has become so powerful a weapon in the hands of the modern archaeologist. Not only the age of the stratum on which it was found, but even the nationality of the maker, can frequently be asserted beyond reasonable question. Every one must be familiar with such statements as that Mycenaean pottery has been found on some site or other recently examined in Greece, Asia Minor, or Palestine. We are led to suppose that there is something distinctive about it which fixes its origin and age quite unmistakably. Now this is not its special fitness for meeting a want which could be met no other way, so that every people everywhere must have produced Mycenaean pottery once they reached the compelling stage of civilization which demanded it. It is some non-essential feature which marks its distinction from all other than deliberate imitations of it. It must be something that appeals to a taste which could only arise after the thing itself had arisen. The admiration felt for Mycenaean pottery would lead to a demand for it, and that might lead to imitation of it, but no conceivable set of circumstances could have led men to achieve it independently. If this could be conceded, the whole science built on modern study of pottery comes to an end. The presence of such pottery in Palestine does not indeed prove that any Mycenaean potter ever visited the country, but that his wares were brought there, were valued and in request. Further, the pottery came within fairly definite limits of time.

Now it is this sort of non-essential, for the most part useless but approved, characteristic which shows conscious imitation, adoption, or adaptation, that proves influence, indebtedness, or copying. In this case instanced, in the absence of all documentary evidence, by its frequency of occurrence, by its adaptation to local circumstance or other local appropriateness, we also fix the locality of its origin. Conclusions of this kind are accepted as legitimate in most modern researches into prehistoric times.

So if we could fasten upon just such a point in the Code of Hammurabi which appears so artificial or arbitrary, so purely local in its character that we cannot imagine it to have independently arisen elsewhere, we could use it as a test case to decide whether the great amount of common matter found in that Code and also the Laws of Moses may be set down as due to common Semitic origin, or to common human genius faced by similar needs. There is no question as to the relative age of the codes to be compared; we know definitely which is older and more original.

Let us then consider a case which, like the need for pottery, might arise anywhere when men had reached the same stage of civilization. A man has lent money to another, or its equivalent in goods. The debtor, as is commonly the case among men, finds himself unable to repay the loan, for he has consumed the goods and been unable to acquire what will replace them. His labour is probably of some value; it should be worth more than his keep; the surplus value, if he can find employment and wages, should in time enable him to repay the debt. Now in his area employment may be scarce, wages low; but at any rate he may offer to work for his creditor. The custom of making such an offer, which differs little from taking service for wages, except that the wage has already been prepaid, may arise almost anywhere. It is probably universal amongst civilized peoples. The creditor soon can count on it as his right to demand his debtor's labour to repay the loan. He probably calculates upon it as his security when he lends, and, if prudent, lends no more than he can reasonably expect to be repaid in this fashion.

Thus far common human experience and its dictates. As a responsible man and the head of his family, the debtor, at least among the Semites, had power over the labour of the other members of his family. There may be peoples where this power does not exist, if so, the power may be called a Semitic trait. But in both the Code of Hammurabi and the Book of the Covenant we have some reason to suppose the debtor would have power to offer not only his own labour but that of his wife, often the better worker of the two, or that of a son or daughter, or of a slave, as well as or instead of his own. Exactly how far his power over the members of his own household extended may be set down, if we chose, as depending upon Semitic custom, if we can show that this extent of power is common to all Semites, at any rate in early times, and is not shared with non-Semitic folk. The parallels in Roman law do show that it did not remain exclusively Semitic, unless it be held that the Twelve Tables were so influenced by Eastern civilization as to have derived this feature ultimately from a Semitic source. It was probably Sumerian also, but there we may perhaps derive it from an early Semitic source. At any rate we do find it common to both Babylonia and Israel, whether they derived it from a common source or obtained it independently.

Now how long shall the debtor or his hostage serve the creditor to pay off the debt? The creditor might well say in the case of a slave, who in practice was often taken as an antichretic pledge for a loan, his labour being supposed to pay the interest on the loan without affecting the capital, that he had a right to keep him always. Theoretically this was true if the loan was about the value of the slave. It would practically be accepting the slave as a payment of the loan. The value of a slave was often very little in excess of the cost of keeping him, feeding, clothing, and housing him. Indeed, he was even an anxiety after he became adult. The owner usually did wisely in providing him with a slave-girl for wife and so breeding a family of slaves, who after they had been kept to adult age might be sold profitably. But even this was a speculation, and at the best not a very profitable business. The creditor who accepted the debtor's slave as a hostage for debt usually took the opportunity of a sale to pass him on. A slave-girl had other uses than her work and was usually more saleable. Hence she was more likely to be accepted and offered as a hostage.

The Code of Hammurabi here steps in with a remarkable set of restrictions upon the freedom of action of the debtor and creditor. The debtor cannot complain if the creditor sells the slave given him as hostage. But if it is a slave-girl who has borne children to the debtor, she cannot be sold. She may be pledged or given to work off a debt, but not alienated by the creditor (§ 118).

If the debtor has handed over wife, son, or daughter as hostage, they have to be treated as freemen still. They are not to forfeit freedom for ever. The Code orders their release at the end of three years' service. It is a noteworthy interference with the above power of a man over his family (§ 116), Semitic or not. In such cases as these there is no account whatever taken of the amount of debt. It is an arbitrary interference on the part of a lawgiver with commercial principles, or selfish instinct, in favour of the weak against the strong. It seems clearly to be an innovation, for though earlier kings had declared amnesty from debt on special occasions, that was a more primitive measure of pity and a generous use of other men's money peculiarly unfair to the soft-hearted lender. This was a bold, calculated move in the direction of humane regulation. It had its risks of abuse, and if Hammurabi had stopped there, he might have done more harm than good. For he would have left it open to the hard-hearted creditor to try and exact more work, the utmost farthing in fact, out of his temporary slave. Accordingly he declared that if the hostage for debt died of blows or want in the creditor's house, the creditor should suffer the same family bereavement as he had brought on the debtor by his cruelty, a regulation which might lead the creditor's family to moderate his exactions, or forfeit the average price of the slave he killed by ill use, and, what the creditor would feel most keenly of all, lose all further claim on the debtor.

Now by such regulations Hammurabi set a very effective limit on two markedly Oriental vices. Men love to gamble by borrowing for present enjoyment on security of some contingent future wealth. They pledge crops, land, houses, family with gleeful irresponsibility. But others are avaricious and only too willing to lend on decent security or even most speculative future profit. Hammurabi's Amorites and Babylonians were by no means above these abuses. He forbade speculation in crops, &c., and by his regulations on these points put a very stringent restraint on debt. The debtor's powers of borrowing were greatly narrowed. A prudent lender found himself checked by the consideration that if the debtor did not pay he would never be able to reclaim more than three years' average work out of the debtor, his wife, son, or daughter. He would have a shrewd guess at what these assets were worth. So the lawgiver cut at the root of much of the misery which his predecessors tried to redress by their slap-dash amnesty.

We do well to remember that a respectable, pious, poor man in Babylonia could usually borrow from his local temple without interest, and that by the Code agricultural loans could not be pressed if the crop failed. Hence we see that most of the debts which Hammurabi made so difficult must have been due to improvidence, laziness, or a weak use of the facility to borrow offered by wealthy, lazy, and avaricious money-lenders.

The Hebrew legislation on the subject is precisely similar save that the term is six years. Whether three or six, the term is so absolutely arbitrary that no possible explanation can be given to account for it. It equally ignores the amount of debt, the value of the debtor's work, and the sacredness of contract. Had both legislations hit upon a three years' term, we might have racked our brains to find a reason why in the world three years should have commended itself to both lawgivers. We should have been tempted to think that these Semites had some sanctity about the term which made it appropriate to select. At any rate we should have wondered what a money-lender in Israel had done to deserve to get twice as much work for his money as the Babylonian. Some might even have been tempted to see early evidence of Jewish aptitude for business. Others would doubtless begin to play with the importance of the value seven to the Jewish mind. Then one would begin to see the influence of P. as in the first chapter of Genesis. Unfortunately the Babylonians of the Hammurabi period had about as much reverence for seven as for three, and perhaps as much for both as the Israelite in the Book of the Covenant.

But it is a poor compliment to a lawgiver of any age to suppose that sacred numbers influenced the nature of his laws.   Doubtless the Jubilee release was economically an advance on sporadic amnesty, but to make a debtor's lot twice as hard and a money-lender's security double, especially as there is no reason to suppose that in Israel the temple was the poor man's bank, all for sake of seven is not a fair charge against Moses or any lawgiver unless it is absolutely certain. The change from three to six is not easy to account for on scientific sociological grounds.

But one of the Hebrew Scriptures does attempt to account for the change, and evidently regards it as a change to be accounted for. The Deuteronomic writer argues that the creditor ought not to deem it hard that he should release his debtor at the end of six years because he had so served a double term.   We may note that as it now stands the text says ' double the hire of a hireling '.   That is purely irrelevant.   A slave's value was surely less to the holder, not more than that of a hireling, for his keep had to be subtracted, and his work was hardly likely to be so valuable as that of a freeman.   The profit of a hireling is the excess of the value of his work above what is paid for it.   The hire of a hireling was surely not just half the value of his own work or of a slave's work.   Indeed, it is not easy to see what the double of a hireling's hire has to do with the question.   The writer was right in saying the term of six years was double something, and there can be no question that it was double three years, and therefore double the term fixed by Hammurabi five hundred or more years before.   The creditor seems to have resented letting the debtor go at all, at any rate till he had worked off all his debt.   The writer clearly knew that the creditor had already obtained twice what he had to expect under other circumstances, and believed he would admit the fact.   It was double the Babylonian allowance.

Can this undesigned coincidence be accidental ?   Is either Semitic custom or human experience competent to explain the significance of the doubleness being pointed out in this way ?

If Canaanite custom before the Exodus had a term of three years' service in such cases, the same as the Hammurabi Code, surely that was due to Babylonian law, unless, as some would maintain, the Amorite dynasty to which Hammurabi belonged really came from Canaan, in which case Hammurabi imposed Canaanite law on

Babylonia. It was a non-essential, anyway; it could nowhere have been the outcome of special circumstances likely to occur again. It was not a creditor's law, for he obviously wanted liberty to keep the debtor's hostage till he had satisfied his own desires; it was not a debtor's law, for he would have surely preferred the three years' limit. It was a concession to the creditor to meet that hard-hearted person's wishes.

It is not the large stock of common matter in the two legislations about a hostage for debt but the disguised yet undeniable adaptation which seems so significant.

Let us now consider another somewhat different case. Death by burning is a horrible punishment, and was so recognized by the later Jewish lawyers, who contrived a legal fiction to do away with its literal infliction even on the scandalous criminals for whom it was intended. Hammurabi orders it twice. It would be very difficult to account by common Semitic custom or evolutionary methods for its being inflicted, if at all, only twice. Yet the laws of Moses inflict it twice also. If these arose independently, what is there from any intelligible point of view to demand its infliction at all—but, if at all, why twice and only twice? And that too in laws so similar?

Well now, in both laws the incest of mother and son is one case. The heinousness of that crime may suffice to justify the hideous penalty. Hammurabi (§§ 157–8) clearly distinguishes incest with a man's own mother and with a step-mother. Leviticus (xx. 14; xxi. 9) makes a curious specification of the case; whether to include other cases or not is not very clear. But evidently this great crime met the same unique punishment.

Hammurabi's second case is that of a votary, or vestal virgin, who left her cloister to open a wineshop or frequent it for strong drink. At first sight we might regard this as a protest against a vestal's intemperance solely. But women did keep wineshops, and their conduct of them is regulated by the Code. We may recall the case of Rahab in Joshua ii. 1. The second case in Hebrew law is Lev. xxi. 9: the priest's daughter who is unchaste is to be burned with fire. Now why are other women of the priest's family not included? Is priest's daughter to be taken, like the *mârat amêlim* in the Code, to mean a woman of the priestly family? Or is it simply a priestess? Surely it is just a periphrasis, perhaps once a gloss on a word become obsolete, for a vowed woman like Jephthah's daughter. There is at first sight not much likeness between the two second cases. But this one evidently puzzled the Jewish commentators, who probably had a traditional knowledge of the real meaning. First Josephus explains the crime not as mere unchastity but as ' opening a tavern '. Was he thinking of Rahab the tavern-keeper who was also a harlot? Or had he an inkling that the crime was the same as Hammurabi had in view? The association of the tavern with immorality was close in Old Testament ideas. Perhaps Hammurabi also had it in mind, for unchastity would be specially revolting in a vestal virgin. Surely the priest's daughter also was a votary. The Rabbis of the Talmud evidently suspected something disguised in the text, for they make a comment upon it which is truly surprising if the text be taken literally. They ask, Shall not a priestess or priest's daughter be treated better than a tavern-keeper? They too knew that in some cases a tavern-keeper had to be burned. We ask, Why and where, if she were not also a vowed woman and in the Hammurabi Code? We need not assume that either Josephus or they had read or heard of Hammurabi's Code, or would have regarded it with anything but detestation if they had. All the more suggestive is it that these learned men should regard the verse as meaning just what that Code did mean.

These points are like the meaningless but obviously Egyptian symbols, often used for decorative purposes on seals, found in Syrian or Hittite seals, which show the influence of the Nile and are never disputed as due to copying, though no longer understood and used for decorative purposes solely.

Some scholars are inclined to attach even more importance to the singular likenesses in literary form, and above all to the disposition of both the Code and the Book of the Covenant in groups of five or ten.

It may be remembered in this connexion that according to the author of the Acts of the Apostles Moses was traditionally learned in all the learning of the Egyptians. Taking that statement as literally true, we now know from the Tell-el-Amarna tablets that that learning included the knowledge of cuneiform at least on the part of some Egyptian scribes before the Exodus. Philo tells us that Moses was also learned in the learning of the Assyrians who were correspondents of Egypt in the same period, of the Babylonians who wrote to the same kings at the same time, and the Chaldeans, who were then known as an independent kingdom in the Southern Sea lands of Babylonia. These and similar traditions are usually dismissed by critics as mere senseless attempts to enhance the reputation of Moses for wisdom and knowledge, which included that of the wisest nations of antiquity. But in view of what we have seen already may there not have been a different reason for these claims? Did not these learned men, who themselves knew much of that knowledge, recognize in the Books of Moses many startling parallels to the wisdom of Babylonia? Was it not the only acceptable way to account for such parallels to assert boldly that Moses did know these things, but in such a way that, guided by God, he used them so far as they were in accordance with Divine revelation; independently indeed as exercising his own discretion in selecting from them, but dependently in so far as they had found out already by man's wisdom or the light of nature that which was good and of good report?

APPENDIX

APPENDIX

SURVEY OF THE BIBLIOGRAPHY OF THE LITERATURE RELATING TO THE CODE OF HAMMURABI.

I. Anticipations of a Babylonian Code of Laws.

In 1890, F. E. Peiser published in his thesis *Iurisprudentiae Babylonicae quae supersunt* (Cöthen, P. Schettler's Erben) a number of fragments of Babylonian Codes of Laws, and aptly illustrated them by relevant legal documents. In 1902, Br. Meissner published what proved to be some fragments of the Code of Hammurabi, from copies made for Ashurbanipal's Library at Nineveh, now preserved in the British Museum. These appeared in the Third Volume of the *Beiträge zur Assyriologie* (Leipzig, Hinrichs, 1898), under the title *Altbabylonische Gesetze* (pp. 473–523), and were commented upon by Fr. Delitzsch in the next volume (pp. 78–87) in an article entitled *Zur juristischen Litteratur Babyloniens* and regarded as *Bruchstücke eines altbabylonischen bürgerlichen Gesetzbuchs.* Judging from the early forms of words and the old Babylonian measures used in these texts the writer called the laws the Code Hammourabi (1902). In his lecture before the German Emperor, which created so much stir in theological circles and excited such general interest in Germany and then over the whole world, Fr. Delitzsch stated that Hammurabi, after his conquest of Elam and expulsion of the Elamite power from Babylonia, was able to promulgate a great *Gesetzessammlung*, which should unify the civilizations of the united kingdom and fix the *bürgerliche Recht* in all essential points. *Babel und Bibel* (Leipzig, Hinrichs, p. 25, 1902 : delivered Jan. 13).

II. The Actual Code

was first published by V. Scheil in the Fourth Volume of the *Mémoires de la Délégation en Perse*, pp. 11–162, with transcriptions, translation, and some notes (Paris, E. Leroux, 1902). Fragments of a second example of the Stele were also given by V. Scheil in the Tenth Volume of the *Mémoires*, pp. 81–84 (1908).

All subsequent editions of the text are based upon this edition. The original monument being now in the Louvre at Paris and a superb cast of it in the Babylonian Room of the British Museum, it is open to any competent scholar to appreciate the extraordinary accuracy of V. Scheil's work. The transcription and translation have naturally been somewhat improved by the intensive study devoted to them by the many scholars who have worked upon the text, especially as the result of comparison with the contemporary legal documents. But the highest praise must be awarded to the genius which so successfully accomplished such a task as that of editing an entirely new text involving so many new words and expressions and such unexpected subjects.

RE-EDITIONS OF THE CUNEIFORM TEXT ITSELF.

Having published an important article on *The Chirography of the Hammurabi Code* in the *American Journal of Semitic Languages and Literatures*, vol. xx, pp. 137–48 (Chicago University Press, 1904), R. F. HARPER proceeded to issue a revised edition of the cuneiform text, with a transcription, a new translation, vocabulary, indexes, and list of signs, under the title *The Code of Hammurabi* (Chicago University Press, 1904), which forms a most convenient student's handbook for English readers.

In 1909, A. UNGNAD published *Keilschrifttexte der Gesetze Hammurapis, Autographie der Stele sowie der altbabylonischen, assyrischen und neubabylonischen Fragmente* (Leipzig, Hinrichs).

Codex Hammurabi. Textus primigenius, transcriptio, translatio, Latina, vocabularia, tabula comparationis inter leges Mosis et Hammurabi. Ad usum privatum auditorum, by A. DEIMEL (Rome, Vatican Press, 1910), has the advantage of a language specially fitted to rendering exactly the turns of expression occurring in the original.

There are some fragments of a copy found at Nippur, now preserved in the Museum at Constantinople, copied by ST. LANGDON, and noticed by him and V. SCHEIL in *Comptes rendus de l'Académie des Inscriptions* (Paris, A. Picard), 1912, p. 159, as *Tablette du Musée de Constantinople contenant les* §§ 145–80 *du Code de Hammourabi* ; and there are other still unpublished copies.

A. POEBEL, in the *Museum Journal of the Philadelphia Museum*, vol. iv, no. 2, 1913, pp. 49–50, announces a further copy of the Code from Nippur, which also supplies some of the missing laws. The fine picture of this tablet shows its present state.

III. TRANSCRIPTIONS AND TRANSLATIONS.

Many works appeared which took V. SCHEIL's transcription and translation as sufficient, only varying from it where the author was already possessed of independent knowledge, or had worked over the text with a view to improve the renderings.

H. WINCKLER, in November, 1902, set out *Die Gesetze Hammurabis, Königs von Babylon um 2250 v. Chr.* as Part 4 of Volume IV of *Der alte Orient* (Leipzig, Hinrichs), a complete translation with valuable introduction and short useful notes. It was followed by a second and third revised editions in March and November, 1903, which called the Code *Das älteste Gesetzbuch der Welt*. In 1904 appeared a fuller work by the same author, *Die Gesetze Hammurabis, Umschrift und Überset-*

zung, dazu Einleitung, Wörter-, Eigennamen-Verzeichnis, die sogenannten sumerischen Familiengesetze und die Gesetztafel, Brit. Mus., 82–7–14, 988. This was a most valuable work, and has been liberally made use of by subsequent writers (Leipzig, Hinrichs).

In 1903 D. H. MÜLLER delivered lectures on the Code embodied in *Vorläufige Mitteilungen über die Gesetze des Hammurabi*, published in the *Anzeiger der philosophisch-historischen Classe der K. K. Akademie der Wissenschaften zu Wien*, vol. xiv, and in the X. *Jahresbericht der israelitisch-theologischen Lehranstalt in Wien*, 1903, issued *Die Gesetze Hammurabis und die mosaische Gesetzgebung*, afterwards published as a separate work (Vienna, A. Hölder, 1903), with some additions. It contained not only a transcription, but a remarkable translation into Hebrew, which did much to bring out the likeness to the laws of Moses, and made the Code accessible to a variety of deeply interested readers who would have missed the point of a transcription, or even of a translation into modern German. It was severely attacked by KOHLER and PEISER in the *Deutsche Literatur-Zeitung*, 1904, no. 5. MÜLLER replied in no. 8, where KOHLER answered him. MÜLLER, however, made many acute suggestions as to the Babylonian text, as well as the subject-matter, and his views have received continued support. His comparison with the other ancient codes, especially with the books of Moses and the Roman Twelve Tables, was full of fresh matter and well deserves careful study.

In 1904 was published what promised to be an epoch-making work. J. KOHLER, Professor of Comparative Law in the University of Berlin, brought his unrivalled knowledge of ancient laws to bear on the legal side of the Code ; and F. E. PEISER, so well versed in Babylonian Legal Documents (see p. 83, below), who had worked with KOHLER before, attempted an improved translation. The work appeared as Band I of *Hammurabi's Gesetze*, and contained *Übersetzung, juristische Wiedergabe, Erläuterung* (Leipzig, Pfeiffer). Band II was to contain philological researches, a transcription with a grammatical and lexicographical treatment. Band III was to be an *Urkundenbuch*, to give a selection of the more important documents of the Hammurabi period so as to form a contemporary commentary. In many points PEISER, or his translation, misled KOHLER, and the work was vigorously attacked by D. H. MÜLLER as *Die Kohler-Peisersche Hammurabi-Übersetzung* in the *Zeitschrift für die Privat- und Öffentlichen Rechte der Gegenwart*, Bd. xxxi (Wien, Hölder, 1904). M. SCHORR also contributed an article on *Die Kohler-Peisersche Hammurabi-Übersetzung* to the *Wiener Zeitschrift für die Kunde des Morgenlandes*, vol. xviii, pp. 208–40, with a long series of acute and severe criticisms. We may note here MÜLLER's *Zur Hammurabi-Kritik* in *Zeitschrift der Deutschen Morgenländischen Gesellschaft*, lix, pp. 145–9, ZIMMERN's article under same title, same place, pp. 150–4, and MÜLLER's article with the same title in *Wiener Zeitschrift für die Kunde des Morgenlandes*, xix, pp. 371–88, carrying on a controversy which cleared up some points. In this great work

A. UNGNAD became associated with KOHLER, and to him is due the *Umschrift* published as Band II with a complete glossary of the Code, and an *Anhang* with a register of the duplicates then known, Old Babylonian, Assyrian, and Neo-Babylonian, which were used to complete the text (Leipzig, Pfeiffer, 1909).

IV. TRANSLATIONS ALONE.

Of translations there was early no lack. SCHEIL's appeared in October, 1902, WINCKLER's first, the following month. *The Oldest Code of Laws in the World*, a baldly literal translation of the Code alone, with a short introduction and index of subjects by C. H. W. JOHNS, appeared in February, 1903 (T. & T. Clark, Edinburgh).

Le leggi di Hammurabi re di Babilonia (a. 2285–2242 a. C.) con prefazione e note, by P. BONFANTE (Milano, 1903), and *Il codice di Hammurabi e la Bibbia*, by FR. MARI (Roma, Desclée, 1903), witness to the interest shown in Italy.

In the *New York Independent* for December 11, 18, 1902, and January 8, 15, 22, 1903, W. HAYES WARD gave a translation of the Code, following WINCKLER closely; as did C. F. KENT in his article, *The Recently Discovered Civil Code of Hammurabi*, published in the *Biblical World* (Chicago University Press, March, 1903).

A translation of the Code also appeared in W. ST. CHAD BOSCAWEN's *The First of Empires*, along with comments and notes. The book presented a clear and readable account of the life and times of Hammurabi and the dynasty to which he belonged. It gave many interesting views upon Babylonian history and the relations to Israelite legislation; but it must be used with great caution, as it is often inaccurate and full of misprints (London and New York, Harper's, 1903).

The many criticisms which had appeared on his first translation and the desirability of a less expensive presentation led V. SCHEIL, in 1903, to put out a fresh translation as *La loi de Hammurabi* (Paris, E. Leroux); in which, however, he accepted little from his critics. A second edition came out in 1904.

Other translations have appeared in connexion with particular discussions. Thus the present writer was induced to set out a fresh translation for his *Babylonian and Assyrian Laws, Contracts, and Letters* in the *Library of Ancient Inscriptions* (Edinburgh, T. & T. Clark, 1904). This work covered most of the helps to the study of the subjects referred to in this survey available up to that date. R. W. ROGERS included an excellent translation and transliteration of the text in his useful work, *Cuneiform Parallels to the Old Testament* (Oxford, Clarendon Press, 1912).

Several of those who have discussed the relation of the Code to the laws of Moses have given translations based upon SCHEIL, WINCKLER, or MÜLLER. *The Hammurabi Code and the Sinaitic Legislation*, by CHILPERIC EDWARDS (London, Watts & Co., 1904), *The Codes of Hammurabi and*

Moses, W. W. DAVIES (New York, Eaton & Maine, 1905), *The Code of Hammurabi*, by C. H. W. JOHNS, in the Extra Volume of *A Dictionary of the Bible* (Edinburgh, T. & T. Clark, 1904), pp. 584–612, may be named. In the second and third editions of his excellent work, *The Old Testament in the Light of the Historical Records and Legends of Assyria and Babylonia* (London, S. P. C. K., 1903), T. G. PINCHES translated the Code (1903, pp. 487–536; 1908, pp. 487–538). The treatment is full of acute observation and accurate scholarship.

A. UNGNAD has contributed a fresh translation to *Altorientalische Texte und Bilder zum alten Testamente, herausgegeben von* H. GRESSMANN, *erster Band*, pp. 140–71 (Tübingen, J. C. B. Mohr, 1909).

V. DISCUSSIONS.

All the above works contained more or less discussion of the Code from various points of view.

In October, 1902, the present writer read a paper before the *Cambridge Theological Society*, an abstract of which appeared in the January number of the *Journal of Theological Studies* (Oxford, Clarendon Press, 1903). The Code was here dealt with as *material for comparison with the Laws of Moses*, but no comparison was made. A. UNGNAD wrote *Zur Syntax der Gesetze Hammurabis* in vol. xvii of the *Zeitschrift für Assyriologie*, pp. 353–78 (Strassburg, K. J. Trübner, May, 1903), and again in vol. xviii, pp. 1–67. The text of the Code, by its careful phraseology and exact use of grammatical forms, has become a classic for the study of the language. The order of the sentence is, however, somewhat unusual, and probably shows the influence of the legal phraseology of the time, which was based on Sumerian law precedents. D. H. MÜLLER took up this point in *Die Wortfolge bei Hammurabi und die sumerische Frage*, an article in *Wiener Zeitschrift für die Kunde des Morgenlandes*, vol. xvii, pp. 337–42 (Wien, Hölder, 1904), followed by *Noch einmal die Wortfolge bei Hammurabi und die sumerische Frage*, vol. xviii, pp. 89–94. *Der Gebrauch der Modi in den Gesetzen Hammurabis*, xviii, pp. 95–8, by D. H. MÜLLER, appeared in the *Wiener Zeitschrift für die Kunde des Morgenlandes* (Vienna, A. Hölder, 1904).

In the *Zeitschrift für Assyriologie*, vol. xviii, pp. 202–22, S. DAICHES contributed a most important article, *Zur Erklärung des Hammurabi-Codex* (1904). The same title was used by A. UNGNAD for an article in the *Wissenschaftliches Correspondenzblatt der Philologie—Novitates* for October, 1906, pp. 8–9.

In vol. xix of the *Zeitschrift für Assyriologie*, pp. 388–91, CHR. SARAUW took up the grammar of the Code in an article *Zum Kasus-System des Hammurabi-Kodex*, 1906.

E. WOHLFRAMM has since written *Untersuchungen zur Syntax des Codex Hammurabis* (Leipzig, Drugulin, 1910).

In the *Expository Times*, vol. xiv, pp. 257–8, the present writer gave an article on the *Code of Hammurabi*, and in *The Journal of Theological Studies*, vol. v, pp. 313–16, under the same title, a notice of the bibliography at that date. A. W. SAYCE wrote on *The Laws of Hammurabi, Expository Times*, vol. xv, pp. 184–6. *The Code of King Hammurabi* appeared in *The Times*, April 14, 1903; *The Laws of Hammurabi*, by L. T. HOBHOUSE, in *The Speaker*, March 7, 1903; D. O. DYKES in *The Juridical Review*, discussed some legal points; E. KÖNIG gave an estimate in *Beweis des Glaubens*, 1903, pp. 169–80. P. LOTICHIUS wrote *Die Gesetzessammlung des Königs Hammurabi von Babylon* in *Protestantenblatt*, 1903, nos. 29, 30. C. F. LEHMANN contributed an article on *Hammurabi's Code* to *The Nineteenth Century*, 1903, pp. 1035–44. These served to give a wider publicity to the Code.

In *Notes on the Hammurabi Monument, Journal of the American Oriental Society*, vol. xxv, pp. 266–78, D. G. LYON, 1904 (New Haven, Conn.), and in *Notes on the Code of Hammurabi, American Journal of Semitic Languages and Literatures*, vol. xxii, pp. 1–28, R. F. HARPER (Chicago, University Press, 1905) made some important contributions to the understanding of the text. D. H. MÜLLER wrote *Ueber die Gesetze Hammurabis* (Wien, Hölder, 1904); T. G. PINCHES had an article *Hammurabi's Code of Laws* in the *Proceedings of the Society of Biblical Archaeology*, 1902, pp. 301–8, among other valuable comments pointing out a hitherto unrecognized fragment in Ashurbanipal's Library. The present writer discussed some difficulties in *Notes on the Code of Hammurabi* contributed to the *American Journal of Semitic Languages and Literature*, vol. xix, pp. 96–107, 172–5 (Chicago, University Press, 1903); T. G. PINCHES wrote also on *The Laws of the Babylonians as recorded in the Code of Hammurabi* in *The Journal of the Victoria Institute*, 1903, pp. 237–55.

P. CRUVEILHIER discussed *Le Code de Hammurabi* in *Revue du Clergé français*, 1912, pp. 413 ff.

There is not space to chronicle all the reviews of these books and articles on the Code, though many of them are practically articles in themselves and marked advances. As a rule, later books used up all that appeared in the reviews of any note, and some of them give references to such sources. Such discussions are of fundamental importance for the exact understanding of the Code.

SEPARATE SECTIONS.

Many discussions arose as to the meaning of particular sections. Thus C. F. LEHMANN(-HAUPT) wrote in *Klio*, vol. iii, pp. 32–41 (1904), on *Ein missverstandenes Gesetz Hammurabis*, which was also taken as the title of an article by F. E. PEISER in *Orientalistische Litteraturzeitung*, vol. vii, cols. 236–7 (1904). Neither of these scholars can be said to have quite settled the questions they had raised; but the subject of §§ 185–93 was greatly cleared by their thoughtful treatment.

In 1908 M. SCHORR contributed to the *Wiener Zeitschrift für die Kunde des Morgenlandes*, vol. xxii, pp. 385–92, an article on *Die §§ 280–282 des Gesetzbuches Hammurabis*, followed, pp. 393–8, by an article of D. H. MÜLLER on *Die §§ 280–282 des Kodex Hammurabis*.

M. SCHORR in 1906 had written in the same journal, vol. xx, pp. 119–23, an article *Zum § 27 des Hammurabi-Gesetzes*, and in the *Vienna Oriental Journal*, xx (1906), pp. 314–36, *Der § 7 des Hammurabi-Gesetzes*.

BR. MEISSNER has discussed the correct word for a builder in the Code in the *Orientalistische Litteraturzeitung*, vol. xv, cols. 38–59 (1912), under the title *Zu Hammurapis Gesetz*, xix, R. 93.

Die Lücke in der Gesetzes-Stele Hammurapis, by A. UNGNAD, in the *Beiträge zur Assyriologie*, vi, Heft 5, discussed all the means known to fill the gap as existing in the text, but the new sources named on p. 66 above will very likely suffice to complete the text.

THE STRUCTURE OF THE CODE.

Considerable weight may ultimately have to be laid on the grouping of the laws by 'tens' or 'fives'. This aspect had been discussed by D. G. LYON in the *Journal of the American Oriental Society*, vol. xxv, pp. 248–65, as *The Structure of the Hammurabi Code* (New Haven, Conn., 1904).

C. F. KENT in his excellent work on *Israel's Laws and Legal Precedents* (London, Hodder & Stoughton, 1907) makes considerable use of a division of Hebrew laws into groups of five or ten, of which the Ten Commandments forms a well-known example. Whether or no these divisions command general assent, we should notice that D. G. LYON finds repeated evidence of the same grouping in the Code of Hammurabi. This naturally cannot be pressed too far as evidence of dependence. But it is surely non-essential that laws should be arranged in pentads unless we are to suppose that a reference to five fingers as a method of recalling the separate clauses is involved, and would be natural to expect in such cases. But that Israelite fondness for the number seven, shown in their seven-day week as against the Babylonian week of five days, or their partiality for other sacred numbers, did not affect the numbering of the laws may well be significant. If it turn out that these groups of five also correspond in contents, even though they show traces of change, we have a strong argument for dependence which supports any others pointing in the same direction.

THE PLACE OF THE CODE IN COMPARATIVE LAW.

As early as October and November, 1902, there appeared *Le Code Babylonien d'Hammourabi* in the *Journal des Savants* (Paris, Hachette), by R. DARESTE, giving a luminous account of the subject-matter of the Code, illustrating it by comparison with a number of ancient legislations. He, of course, based his conclusions entirely upon SCHEIL's translation, but his work still remains most valuable. In 1903 appeared SCHMERSAHL'S *Das älteste Gesetzbuch der Welt : Die Gesetze Hammurabis* in the *Deutsche Juristen-Zeitung*, pp. 111 ff. R. DARESTE also published *Le Code Babylonien d'Hammourabi* in the *Nouvelle Revue historique de droit français et étranger* (Paris, Larose, January and February, 1903). *Hammurapi und das Salische Recht*, by H. FEHR (Bonn, Marcus & Weber, 1910), is a very remarkable study.

A first-rate work was G. COHN's lecture, *Die Gesetze Hammurabis* (Zürich, Füssli, 1903). KOHLER and MÜLLER (see pp. 67, 69) have to be weighed.

C. STOOSS in his article *Das babylonische Strafrecht Hammurabis, Schweizerische Zeitschrift für Strafrecht*, vol. xvi (Basel, Georg, 1903), took up the question of 'Crimes and Punishments', on which see also the article with that title by T. G. PINCHES in *The Encyclopaedia of Religion and Ethics*, iv, pp. 256 ff.; and *Imprisonment*, by the same author, iv, pp. 260 ff. *Die peinlichen Strafen im Kriegs- und Rechtswesen der Babylonier und Assyrer*, by J. JELITTO (Breslau, 1913), adds considerably to the subject. Compare also *Zum ältesten Strafrecht der Kulturvölker*, by TH. MOMMSEN and others (Leipzig, Duncker, 1905).

The judicial procedure remains in many points obscure despite the fine *Essai sur l'organisation judiciaire de la Chaldée à l'époque de la première dynastie babylonienne*, by ED. CUQ, in the *Revue d'Assyriologie*, 1910, pp. 65–101, which records most known facts; *Commentaire juridique d'un jugement sous Ammiditana*, by the same author in the same journal, 1910, pp. 129–38; and again *Un procès criminel à Babylone sous le règne de Samsou-iluna*, 1911, pp. 173–81. P. DHORME discussed in the same volume, p. 99, *Un appel sous Samsou-iluna. A Legal Episode in Ancient Babylonian Family Life*, in the *Proceedings of the Society of Biblical Archaeology*, 1910, pp. 81–92, 129–42, is by W. T. PILTER.

The tenure of land was elucidated by H. WINCKLER in *Zum babylonisch-chaldäischen Feudalwesen*, in *Altorientalische Forschungen*, i, pp. 497–503. *La Propriété foncière en Chaldée*, by ED. CUQ (Paris, Larose, 1907), chiefly deals with later developments; as do the articles by J. OPPERT, *Le droit de retrait lignager à Ninive* in the *Comptes rendus* of the *Académie des inscriptions et belles-lettres* (Paris, 1898), and *Das assyrische Landrecht* in the *Zeitschrift für Assyriologie*, xiii, pp. 243–76 (Weimar, 1898).

The position of some classes or castes named will be dealt with under the LEXICOGRAPHY OF THE CODE, pp. 74 ff. *The Consecrated Women of the Hammurabi Code* is an important essay by D. G. LYON in the *Studies in the History of Religions presented to Crawford Howell Toy* (New York, The Macmillan Co., 1912), pp. 341–60. See also *Altbabylonische Rechtsurkunden aus der Zeit der Hammurabi-Dynastie*, by S. DAICHES (Leipzig, Hinrichs, 1903).

The view of law as sworn contract has importance enough to be specially considered. It was early discovered in the so-called contracts which were once regarded as legal decisions. We may refer to *Sworn Obligations under Egyptian and Babylonian Law*, by E. and V. REVILLOUT, and *Sworn Obligations in Babylonian Law* by the same authors in *The Babylonian and Oriental Record*, vol. i, no. 7, and vol. ii, no. 1. A. UNGNAD pointed out *Eine neue Form der Beglaubigung in altbabylonischen Urkunden* in the *Orientalistische Litteraturzeitung*, 1906, cols. 163–4. The whole subject was taken up by S. A. B. MERCER in his dissertation on *The Oath in Babylonian and Assyrian Literature* (Munich, 1911).

The idea underlying the appeal to the ordeal is closely allied to that of the oath, and F. E. PEISER wrote *Zum Ordal bei Babyloniern* in the *Orientalistische Litteraturzeitung*, 1911, cols. 477–9.

The importance of the family in the Code and Babylonian Law in general has led to several monographs. *Le Mariage à Babylone*, by ED. CUQ (Paris, Lecoffre, 1905), and *Zur Terminologie im Eherecht bei Hammurabi*, by D. H. MÜLLER, in the *Wiener Zeitschrift für die Kunde des Morgenlandes*, xix, pp. 352–8, deal chiefly with the Code. L. FREUND'S *Zur Geschichte des Ehegutrechtes bei den Semiten* (Vienna, A. Hölder, 1909) chiefly deals with Jewish custom. *Liebe und Ehe im alten Orient*, by F. FREIHERR VON REITZENSTEIN (Stuttgart, Franckh, 1909), devotes pp. 51 to 70 to the Babylonian side. Of course, W. ROBERTSON SMITH'S *Kinship and Marriage* will be consulted in its new edition by S. A. COOK (London, A. & C. Black, 1903).

Closely connected are other questions as to the status of women. Already in 1892 J. OPPERT was able to make out much about *Liberté de la femme à Babylone* in the *Revue d'Assyriologie*, ii, pp. 89–90. V. MARX discussed *Die Stellung der Frauen in Babylonien* in the *Beiträge zur Assyriologie*, iv, pp. 1–77.

Slavery in Babylonia was very different from either Roman or modern ideals. As long ago as 1888 J. OPPERT had made out much from the legal documents of later times in his article *La condition des esclaves à Babylone* in the *Comptes rendus* of the *Académie des inscriptions et belles-lettres* for that year. BR. MEISSNER had written a dissertation in 1882, *De servitute babylonico-assyriaca* (Leipzig), which still deserves to be consulted. M. SCHORR wrote *Arbeitsruhetage im alten Babylonien* in *Revue Sémitique*, 1912, pp. 398–9.

The questions of guarantee, security, &c., are finely treated by P. KOSCHAKER in his work, *Babylonisch-assyrisches Bürgschaftsrecht* (Leipzig, Teubner, 1911).

Business in general is well dealt with by FR. DELITZSCH in his *Handel und Wandel in Altbabylonien* (Stuttgart, Deutsche Verlagsanstalt, 1910). *Die Commenda im islamischen Rechte*, by J. KOHLER (Würzburg, Stahel, 1885), is to be compared.

Aus dem altbabylonischen Recht, by BR. MEISSNER, in *Der alte Orient*, vii, Heft 1, 1905 (Leipzig, Hinrichs), is excellent.

On the whole subject of Babylonian law a valuable treatise is P. KOSCHAKER's article, *The Scope and Methods of a History of Assyrio-*

Babylonian Laws in the *Proceedings of the Society of Biblical Archaeology*, 1913, pp. 230–43. *Babylonian and Assyrian Laws, Contracts, and Letters*, by the present writer, in *The Library of Ancient Inscriptions* (T. & T. Clark, Edinburgh, 1904), and the articles on *Babylonian Law*, by the same author, in *The Encyclopaedia Britannica*, vol. iii, 1910, may be consulted, pp. 115–21, and in *The Encyclopaedia of Religion and Ethics*. The French jurist, ED. CUQ, in his *Notes d'épigraphie et de papyrologie*, published in the *Nouvelle Revue historique du droit français et étranger* (Paris, L. Larose), 1906–1909, discussed many points of *Le Droit babylonien au temps de la Première Dynastie de Babylone*.

LEXICOGRAPHY OF THE CODE.

Most of the discussions and editions above referred to deal with points in the lexicography. The edition by UNGNAD in his Band II, named on p. 68, gives the latest results of the investigations in this domain. A few other works deserving of note will be added here.

The meaning of *amêlu* was elucidated by H. WINCKLER in his *Altorientalische Forschungen*, ii, pp. 312–15, 1901 (Leipzig, Pfeiffer).

The difficult word *mushkênu*, rendered *noble* by SCHEIL and after him by DARESTE and others, was given this meaning because the fines and penalties inflicted on him in the Code seemed to be less than those inflicted on the ordinary man. The ideogram used in the Code was not rendered into Semitic Babylonian by SCHEIL, but first in print by H. ZIMMERN. A crowd of extraordinary guesses as to the meaning of the term were hazarded, founded on the cognate languages. Thus it was discussed by E. LITTMANN in *Zur Bedeutung von misken, Zeitschrift für Assyriologie*, vol. xvii, pp. 262–5 (Strassburg, K. J. Trübner, 1903), who made it out to be *leper* and by ET. COMBE in *Babyloniaca*, vol. iii, pp. 73–4, who settled the meaning from its use in modern Arabic. The present writer had already anticipated much of this in his *Oldest Code* and the *Notes on the Hammurabi Code*, above, p. 70.

The meaning and status of the *rîdtsâbê* was discussed by S. DAICHES, *Zur Erklärung des Hammurabi-Codex*, in *Zeitschrift für Assyriologie*, 1904–1905, pp. 202–22. Many useful hints will be found in *Semitica : Sprach- und rechtsvergleichende Studien*, in the *Sitzungsberichte der philosophisch-historischen Klasse der kaiserlichen Akademie in Wien*, 1906, cols. 1–88 (Wien, A. Hölder).

The exact way in which the Semitic people of the Hammurabi period exploited the stores of legal knowledge acquired by the Sumerians is still much discussed. So by M. SCHORR in his *Die altbabylonische Rechtspraxis*, published in *Wiener Zeitschrift für die Kunde des Morgenlandes*, vol. xxiv, pp. 431–61, and again in the *Revue Sémitique*, 1912, pp. 378–97, *Zur Frage der semitischen und sumerischen Elemente im altbabylonischen Rechte*. See also *Das Sumerische in den Rechtsurkunden der Hammurabi-Periode*, by M. SCHORR, in the *Hilprecht Anniversary Volume*, pp. 20–32.

The question whether the Sumerian phrases in the contemporary contracts were read as Semitic or Sumerian has been discussed by A. POEBEL in the *Orientalistische Litteraturzeitung*, 1911, cols. 241–7, under the title *Zur Aussprache der sumerischen Phrasen in den altbabylonischen Rechtsurkunden*, and in cols. 373–4 A. UNGNAD wrote, under the same title, *Eine Berichtigung*. M. SCHORR replied, cols. 559–61.

The question how far the Hammurabi Code was operative was soon raised. The existence of a very large number of legal documents relating to all manner of transactions seemed likely to afford a ready answer. In 1905 BR. MEISSNER wrote his *Theorie und Praxis im altbabylonischen Recht* for the *Mitteilungen der Vorder-asiatischen Gesellschaft*, pp. 257–303. The need of a more extended examination made the promise of KOHLER and PEISER's *Hammurabi-Gesetz* so welcome, see p. 67. KOHLER and UNGNAD have now fulfilled this by publishing in Heft III–V the whole available material as *Übersetzte Urkunden* with most valuable *Erläuterungen* (Leipzig, Hinrichs, 1909–1911). A similar enterprise was undertaken by M. SCHORR in *Kodeks Hammurabiego a owczesna praktyka prawna, Das Gesetzbuch Hammurabis und die zeitgenössische Rechtspraxis*, in the *Bulletin de l'Académie des Sciences de Cracovie*, followed by *Altbabylonische Rechtsurkunden aus der Zeit der I. babylonischen Dynastie* in the *Sitzungsberichte der kaiserlichen Akademie der Wissenschaften in Wien, philosophisch-historische Klasse*, 155. Band, 2. Abhandlung, 1907, 160. Band, 5. Abhandlung, 1909, and 165. Band, 2. Abhandlung, 1910 (Vienna, A. Hölder), with transcription, translation, and commentary. Together with UNGNAD's work this should enable any scholar to form a well-founded and independent judgement.

It is natural to inquire what were the laws of that earlier people in Babylonia who preceded the Semites and are now called Sumerians. The Semites took over their legal phrases, see above, and probably with them some of their laws. The Semitic scribes drew up long lists of these Sumerian phrases, many of which they still used in drawing up their legal documents, just as Latin phrases or Norman-French lingered on in our law-books. These phrases they translated, in parallel columns with the Sumerian. Such books of phrases were issued in long series. One such series, usually called *Ana Ittishu*, was discussed by BR. MEISSNER in the *Wiener Zeitschrift für die Kunde des Morgenlandes*, iv, pp. 301 ff. A great deal of it is published by P. HAUPT in vol. i of the *Assyriologische Bibliothek*; by F. HOMMEL in his *Sumerische Lesestücke*; by FR. DELITZSCH in his *Assyrische Lesestücke*, 3rd edition, 1900, pp. 130–2; and by MEISSNER in the *Zeitschrift für Assyriologie*, 1892, vii, pp. 16–32. PINCHES gives an account of it in the *Encyclopaedia of Religion and Ethics*, iv, p. 256, 1910, where he calls it the *Ulutinabishu Series*. Not much law can be made out of this scrappy source; but one tablet records a set of regulations which seem to be extracted from a code. They are usually referred to as *The Sumerian Family Laws*, and are dealt with by T. G. PINCHES in the *Encyclopaedia of Religion and Ethics*, iv, p. 257, 1910, and by JEREMIAS in the same work, v, p. 447. A full treatment by P. HAUPT is *Die sumerischen Familiengesetze in Keilschrift, Transcription und Übersetzung* (Leipzig, 1879). WINCKLER, COOK, PEISER, UNGNAD, and most of the writers on the comparative side have quoted them in their above-named works.

It may be doubted whether the so-called *Warnings to Kings against Injustice*, see T. G. PINCHES in his *Encyclopaedia* article, iv, p. 261, note 1, are so early, or really preserve part of a code. References to legal reforms may be seen in the inscriptions of Urukagina, see L. W. KING's *History of Sumer and Akkad*, pp. 178–84 and the references, but here again we cannot reconstruct much of the Sumerian law in question.

We have noted the discussion, p. 75, of the way in which Semitic scribes regarded the Sumerian phrases they used.

The conclusion that Hammurabi codified the earlier legislation was natural, and similarities in form suggested that he adopted much of the Sumerian law which was previously in force.

A. T. CLAY in the *Orientalistische Litteraturzeitung*, xvii, January, 1914 (Leipzig, Hinrichs), writing on *A Sumerian Prototype of the Hammurabi Code*, has made it clear that some of the laws existed in a Sumerian dress. Hammurabi, as we have already contended, modified the previously existing Sumerian laws, and taking some over bodily, changed others to suit the peculiar prejudices of his subjects and the circumstances of his time. We may soon be able to judge whether CLAY's *Sumerian Code*, as we may call it, was really early, or only the dress in which Hammurabi's law appeared in his Sumerian provinces.

We may pass on to notice briefly the chief sources from which it is possible to deduce much of the local customary law throughout the history of Babylonia. It may formally be divided into Temple accounts and contracts, but a detailed classification would demand much more space than we can here afford.

THE TEMPLE ACCOUNTS.

At all times the great temples of Assyria and Babylonia kept extensive accounts of even daily revenue and expenditure. These accounts were most carefully preserved, being written with special care on well selected clay, and have reached us as a rule in exceptionally fine condition. They give us an immense mass of information, largely consisting of dry and disconnected items, but helping to build up knowledge. The French explorations made by DE SARZEC at Telloh resulted in the discovery of an enormous number of documents, mostly accounts kept of the daily expenses and revenues of the vast temples there, from the earliest times down to the Dynasty of Ur. One huge find of some 30,000 tablets of the latter period were stolen by Arabs, and have been sold in large quantities to European and American Museums, or to private collectors. Few of them are legal documents, or concerned with other than Temple business, but their contents illustrate the state of society in the times before the First Dynasty of Babylon. They are most important for determining the extent to which the Code of Hammurabi was dependent on, or influenced by, the Sumerian Law of earlier days.

Of those which reached Constantinople, the products of the season of 1894 consisted entirely of tablets of the Dynasty of Ur, and were classified by V. SCHEIL. The tablets found in 1895 were catalogued by THUREAU-DANGIN, and are mostly of the Dynasty of Akkad. The finds of 1900 are all of the Dynasty of Ur. These are all now catalogued and largely published in the *Inventaire des Tablettes de Tello conservées au Musée Ottoman* (Paris, E. Leroux, 1910), by FR. THUREAU-DANGIN and H. DE GENOUILLAC.

But by far the largest part of the finds came into the hands of dealers, and so into the museums of Europe and America; and these were published sooner. Thus in 1891 some were reproduced by photography in DE SARZEC's *Découvertes en Chaldée* (Paris, E. Leroux), plate 41. These tablets, preserved in the Louvre, were, however, properly presented by the Sultan. A great many thus acquired were published by THUREAU-DANGIN as *Tablettes chaldéennes inédites* in the *Revue d'Assyriologie*, iv, pp. 69–86 (Paris, E. Leroux, 1897). In the same journal, v, pp. 67–102, 1902, he gave a *Notice sur la troisième collection de tablettes*, and in 1903 published a *Recueil de tablettes chaldéennes* (Paris, E. Leroux), which gave improved editions of the above. Other articles appeared in the *Revue d'Assyriologie*, iii, pp. 118–46 (1895), iv, pp. 13–27 (1897), and in *Comptes rendus de l'Académie des Inscriptions* for 1896, by the same writer, pp. 355–61. These works not only made available large numbers of texts, but also gave most important contributions to their understanding.

In 1896 H. V. HILPRECHT published three of the tablets in the Imperial Ottoman Museum at Constantinople in his *Old Babylonian Inscriptions*, part II, nos. 124–6 (Philadelphia, *Transactions of the American Philosophical Society*).

In *Cuneiform Texts from Babylonian Tablets, etc., in the British Museum*, vols. i, iii, v, vii, ix, x (London, British Museum), copied by L. W. KING, 1896–1900; *Ancient Babylonian Temple Records*, copied by W. R. ARNOLD (New York, Columbia University Press, 1896); *Old Babylonian Temple Records*, are texts copied and discussed by R. J. LAU (New York, Columbia University Press, 1906); *Haverford Library Collection of Cuneiform Tablets or Documents from the Temple Archives of Telloh*, part I, 1905; part II, 1909; part III, 1914 (Philadelphia, J. C. Winston Co.), several hundreds of these texts appeared.

G. REISNER, in 1902, published *Tempelurkunden aus Telloh* (Berlin, W. Spemann), being the collection presented to the Berlin Museum by H. SIMON. H. RADAU in his *Early Babylonian History* (New York, 1903), published and discussed a number purchased for the E. A. Hoffmann collections in the New York Metropolitan Museum. T. G. PINCHES dealt with

Some Case Tablets from Telloh in the *Journal of the Royal Asiatic Society* for 1905, pp. 815–29, and, in 1909, published *The Amherst Tablets*, being an *Account of the Babylonian Inscriptions in the Collection of the Right Honourable Lord Amherst of Hackney, at Didlington Hall, Norfolk* (London, Quaritch). H. DE GENOUILLAC published and discussed some texts of H. SCHLUMBERGER's as *Tablettes d'Ur* in the *Hilprecht Anniversary Volume*, pp. 137–41. In 1911 T. G. PINCHES dealt with some *Tablets from Telloh in Private Collections* in *The Journal of the Royal Asiatic Society*, pp. 1039–62, and ST. LANGDON gave *Some Sumerian Contracts* in the *Zeitschrift für Assyriologie*, 1911, pp. 205–14. V. SCHEIL contributed a series of *Notes d'épigraphie et d'archéologie assyriennes* to the *Recueil de Travaux* (Paris, E. Bouillon), vol. xvii, 1895, pp. 28–30 ; xviii (1896), pp. 64–74 ; xix (1897), pp. 44–64 ; xx (1898), pp. 55–72, 200–10 ; xxi (1899), pp. 26–9, 123–6 ; xxii (1900), pp. 27–39, 78–80, 149–61 ; xxiii (1901), pp. 18–23 ; xxiv (1902), pp. 24–9, in which among other priceless records he gave many extracts from the Telloh texts, some entire texts, and much elucidation of the same. Special studies devoted to the subject are : H. DE GENOUILLAC's *Textes juridiques de l'époque d'Ur* in the *Revue d'Assyriologie*, 1911, pp. 1–32 ; H. DEIMEL's *Studien zu C. T., I, III, V, VII, IX, X*, in the *Zeitschrift für Assyriologie*, 1911, pp. 328–45 ; *Sátilla, textes juridiques de la seconde dynastie d'Our* in *Babyloniaca*, iii, 1910, pp. 81–132, by F. PELÉGAUD, and *Di-tilla, textes juridiques chaldéens de la seconde dynastie d'Our*, by C. H. VIROLLEAUD (Poitiers, A. Boutifard, 1903) ; *Comptabilité chaldéenne*, by the same author, same place and publisher, 1903, is a series of valuable essays. G. A. BARTON gave *A Babylonian Ledger Account of Reeds and Wood* in the *American Journal of Semitic Languages and Literatures*, 1911, pp. 322–7, and in the same journal, 1912, pp. 207–10, another text of the same sort.

Tablets of the same period have been found by the thousand at Jokha, the ancient Umma, for centuries the hereditary foe of Telloh, and at Drehem, which seems to have been a closely dependent city of the Nippur district. They have already found their way in large numbers to Europe and America.

Tablets from Jokha were first noticed by V. SCHEIL in his *Notes d'épigraphie et d'archéologie assyrienne* in *Recueil de Travaux*, vol. xix, pp. 62–3, 1897, who showed that Jokha was Umma. FR. THUREAU-DANGIN in the *Revue d'Assyriologie* (viii), 1911, pp. 152–8, who deals with *Les noms des mois sur les tablettes de Djokha*, gives a number of these texts from the time of the Dynasties of Akkad and Ur. ST. LANGDON has published *A tablet from Umma in the Ashmolean Museum at Oxford* in the *Proceedings of the Society of Biblical Archaeology*, 1913, pp. 47–52. In contents these are very similar to the tablets from Telloh or Drehem, and seem to have been often confused with them by the dealers.

ST. LANGDON published *Tablets from the Archives of Drehem* (Paris, Geuthner, 1912) ; L. DELAPORTE, *Tablettes de Dréhem* in *Revue d'Assyrio-*

logie, 1911, pp. 183–98 ; P. Dhorme, *Tablettes de Dréhem à Jérusalem* in same journal, pp. 39–63 ; H. de Genouillac, *Tablettes de Dréhem, publiées avec inventaire et tables. Musée du Louvre* (Paris, Geuthner, 1911), and *La trouvaille de Dréhem, Étude avec un choix de textes de Constantinople et Bruxelles* (Paris, Geuthner, 1911) ; see also *Some Sumerian Contracts*, by St. Langdon, in the *Zeitschrift für Assyriologie*, 1911, pp. 205–14. A useful summary is *Some Published Texts from Dréhem*, by I. M. Price, in the *American Journal of Semitic Languages and Literatures*, 1912, pp. 211–15.

Sumerian Administrative Documents from the Second Dynasty of Ur, from the Temple Archives of Nippur, vol. iii, part i of Series A, Cuneiform Texts, in *Publications of the Babylonian Expedition of the University of Pennsylvania* (Philadelphia, 1910), deals with closely related texts.

E. Huber wrote *Die altbabylonischen Darlehenstexte aus der Nippur-Sammlung im K. O. Museum in Konstantinopel* as a contribution to the *Hilprecht Anniversary Volume*, pp. 189–222. V. Scheil in his *Notes d'épigraphie* made some entries about those Nippur texts which reached Constantinople, see p. 78.

An allied text was given by P. Dhorme in the *Journal Asiatique*, 1912, pp. 158–9, as *Un brouillon d'inventaire.*

The whole subject of these Temple Records is being studied by H. Torczyner, who has started with *Vorläufige Bemerkungen* to *Altbabylonische Tempelrechnungen, umschrieben und erklärt* in the *Anzeiger der Kaiserlichen Akademie der Wissenschaften in Wien*, 1910, pp. 136–40.

On the general scope and purpose of the Temple Records, see the article on *Babylonian Book-keeping*, by A. T. Clay, in the *American Journal of Archaeology*, 1910, pp. 74 ff.

The very ancient texts from Telloh, usually called Pre-Sargonic, have been issued, beside Thureau-Dangin's *Recueil de Tablettes chaldéennes*, by Allotte de la Fuÿe as *Documents présargoniques* (Paris, E. Leroux, 1908, 1909). *Sumerian Tablets in the Harvard Semitic Museum* was begun, by Mary Ida Hussey, with part 1 in 1912. *Two Tablets of the Period of Lugalanda* were published by St. Langdon in *Babyloniaca*, 1911, pp. 246–7. Much the most useful publication, however, is *Tablettes sumériennes archaïques*, by H. de Genouillac (Paris, Geuthner, 1909), which gives not only texts, but transcriptions and such translation as is possible, and also an admirable account of all they imply, as to law and custom. A considerable amount of this is strikingly like the later laws. In *The Amherst Tablets* (London, Quaritch, 1908), T. G. Pinches published a few more. The bulk of them still await publication.

Ancient Bullae and Seals of Shirpurla by N. P. Likhatscheff, published in the *Imperial Russian Archaeological Society's Classical Section IV*, pp. 225–63, 1907, written in Russian, gives a number of similar tablets. *Oriental Antiquities*, by M. V. Nikolsky, in the *Oriental Commission of the Imperial Moscow Archaeological Society*, iii, Series 2, 1908, has over 300 such texts. These appear to belong to the same period.

Some valuable discussions will be found in *État des décès survenus dans le personnel de la déesse Bau sous le règne d'Urukagina*, by ALLOTTE DE LA FUŸE, in the *Revue d'Assyriologie*, 1910, pp. 139–46.

In his *Recueil de Tablettes chaldéennes* (Paris, E. Leroux, 1903) FR. THUREAU-DANGIN gave as his third series a number of texts of the Sargonic period, dated in the reigns of Shargani-shar-ali and Naram-Sin. A number more are published or described in the *Inventaire des tablettes de Tello conservées au Musée Impérial Ottoman*, Tome I, by THUREAU-DANGIN, 1910, and Tome II, by H. DE GENOUILLAC, 1911, and several other collections are to be published shortly.

The very early texts from the ancient Shuruppak which have reached the Louvre were published by THUREAU-DANGIN in his *Recueil* named above, and in the *Revue d'Assyriologie*, vi (1904), pp. 143–54, he wrote *Contrats archaïques provenant de Shuruppak*, with the intention of deciphering and explaining them as far as possible.

CONTRACT LITERATURE.

Many texts published in the above collections of Temple Accounts are bonds, deeds of sale, even legal decisions, &c., and really come under the head of contracts. But even among the collections of contracts some accounts have been published, and it is scarcely necessary here to quote the same book under both heads.

Curiously enough the first contracts to attract attention were of an early date. LOFTUS found at Senkereh a number of most interesting case-tablets, the principal document being invariably enclosed in a clay envelope which, as was subsequently discovered, was inscribed with an abstract or practical duplicate of the principal document. Many speculations arose as to their purpose. Some regarded them as a substitute for money, or cheques, banknotes in clay (so LAYARD in 1853), and other weird guesses. GEORGE SMITH first recognized their meaning and value for history by publishing their dates, the names which the Babylonians gave to the years, calling them after some prominent event.

Discovered in 1854, they were first published in 1882 by J. N. STRASSMAIER. Owing to some misapprehension, as given in LAYARD's *Nineveh and Babylon*, p. 496, despite the clear statement on pp. 270–72 of LOFTUS, *Travels and Researches in Chaldea and Susiana*, they were called *Die altbabylonischen Verträge aus Warka* in the *Beilage* to the *Verhandlungen des V. internationalen Orientalistischen Congresses zu Berlin*, 1881. They were accompanied by a list of words and names. E. and V. REVILLOUT discussed them most interestingly in *Une Famille de commerçants de Warka*. They proved to be of the time of Hammurabi and his son Samsu-iluna after these kings had expelled Rim-Sin from the South of Babylonia. But there were several dated in the reign of Rim-Sin, and in those of Sin-idinnam and Nûr-adad, kings who had preceded him. Thus they showed how, despite changes of dynasty, the civil life of the subject population went on undisturbed, and customs changed but little.   They show how closely the Code pictures the daily life of the people.   As most illustrative of the Code, constituting a contemporary commentary on its regulations and consisting chiefly of examples of the same cases as there considered, we may here group in order of publication the collections from the First Dynasty of Babylon.

Inscribed Babylonian Tablets in the possession of Sir Henry Peek, Bart., 1888, contained a few texts of this period, copied, transcribed, and translated by T. G. PINCHES.   This made considerable advances, but there was not yet enough material to solve many obscurities.   These tablets came from Sippara.

It was evident that the only hope of understanding such technical documents lay in the publication of further material, so that by comparison of similar passages some information could be obtained as to alternative readings and phrases.

In 1893 a great advance was made by MEISSNER with his *Beiträge zum altbabylonischen Privatrecht* (Leipzig, Hinrichs), which gave a full transliteration and translation of 111 texts, all carefully published in autography.   Full notes and invaluable comments made this a standard work. The texts were chiefly from tablets found at Sippara, and stored in the British Museum, and at Berlin where a large quantity had been purchased. MEISSNER also reproduced some of the Warka texts.

In the fourth volume of SCHRADER's *Keilinschriftliche Bibliothek*, 1896, F. E. PEISER gave a collection of contract texts in transcription and translation, arranged in chronological order.   He included thirty-one texts of this period (Berlin, Reuther and Reichard).   These were called *Texte juristischen und geschäftlichen Inhalts,* and marked a further advance in treatment.   In this year also began the great series of publications called *Cuneiform Texts from Babylonian Tablets, &c., in the British Museum, printed by order of the Trustees.*   Vols. ii, iv, vi, and viii (1896, 1897, 1898, 1899), contain copies of no fewer than 395 texts mostly of this period, a most valuable addition to our knowledge of the subject.   They were from the practised hand of T. G. PINCHES, who gave in the *Journal of the Royal Asiatic Society,* 1897 and 1899, some transliterations and translations with notes and comments on fifteen of them.   They were all Sippara tablets.

In 1902 appeared *Une saison de fouilles à Sippar* (Le Caire, Institut Français), in which V. SCHEIL gave an account of his explorations at Abu Habba, the ancient Sippara, in 1892–1893, and many texts in a preliminary form, with transcription, translation, and comments, thus making known a most valuable supplement to the earlier publications of First Dynasty tablets.

In 1906 TH. FRIEDRICH published in the *Beiträge zur Assyriologie,* vol. v, a number of texts from the tablets found by SCHEIL at Sippara, and then preserved in the Museum at Constantinople, as *Altbabylonische*

Urkunden aus Sippara (Leipzig, Hinrichs), which completed Scheil's work in many ways.

In 1906, A. H. Ranke published *Babylonian Legal and Business Documents from the time of the First Babylonian Dynasty,* as vol. vi, part 1, of the Series A, Cuneiform Texts, of the *Publications of the Babylonian Expedition of the University of Pennsylvania* (Philadelphia, University of Pennsylvania). They probably all came from Sippara, though two may be from Babylon, unless the king was then holding Court in Sippara.

In 1908 J. É. Gautier gave us *Archives d'une famille de Dilbat au temps de la Première Dynastie de Babylon* (Le Caire, Institut Français), with transcriptions and translations of sixty-six tablets from a new site, which the contents of the texts certainly prove to be that of the ancient city of Dilbat. The work was well done, but needed revision by fresh material.

About this time native diggers brought to light fresh material from several new sites. Especially valuable were the texts from Kish, Larsa, Opis, Babylon, and Shittab. These were eagerly acquired by the various Museums, and shortly gave rise to a crop of fresh publications.

In 1909 came *Babylonian Legal and Business Documents from the time of the First Dynasty of Babylon,* by A. Poebel, being vol. vi, part 2, of Series A, Cuneiform Texts, of the *Publications of the Babylonian Expedition of the University of Pennsylvania* (Philadelphia, University of Pennsylvania). Again a fresh site, the ancient Nippur, yielded its contribution. Here most of the tablets exhibit the old Sumerian phraseology.

A. Ungnad published, in 1909, a large number of texts from tablets in the Berlin Museum, acquired at various dates. They appeared as vols. vii, viii, ix of the *Vorderasiatische Denkmäler* (Leipzig, Hinrichs). Most of them undoubtedly came from Sippara; one from Der ez-Zor, near the Chabour, and those in vol. vii from Dilbat, apparently the modern Delam. Thus we can again compare contemporary documents from a fresh site, which proves to have been influenced by other peoples, the Mitanni, Elamites, &c. In *Urkunden aus Dilbat,* vol. vi, part 5, of the *Beiträge zur Assyriologie* (Leipzig, Hinrichs, 1909), A. Ungnad transcribes, translates, and comments upon the large collection of letters and contracts which had been published from Dilbat. His works brought a large amount of most valuable information for the period.

In 1910 Thureau-Dangin issued *Lettres et contrats de l'époque de la Première dynastie babylonienne* (Paris, Geuthner), a most valuable work for its indexes, as well as the interesting texts. A long and extremely fine text was also given by him as *Un jugement sous Ammiditana,* in *Revue d'Assyriologie,* 1910, pp. 121–7. Here were texts from Sippara, Babylon, Dilbat, Kish, and possibly Shittab, as well as some more from Der-ez-Zor. In the *Revue d'Assyriologie,* 1911, pp. 68–79, Thureau-Dangin published *Sept contrats* of the reigns of the kings of Kish, who were contemporary with the foundation of the First Dynasty and themselves Amorites.

St. Langdon published several more of these *Tablets from Kish* in the *Proceedings of the Society of Biblical Archaeology*, 1911, pp. 185–96, and in the same journal for 1912, pp. 109–13, gave eleven *Contracts from Larsa*.

C. E. Keiser published *Tags and Labels from Nippur* in *The Museum Journal of Philadelphia*, vol. iii, no. 2, pp. 29–31. These closely related documents form a borderland between contracts and accounts.

These contracts are so much more important for the elucidation of the Code than any later documents that we may now notice the chief discussions of them.

Not much of this class of documents has yet come to light for the Third or Kassite Dynasty of Babylon. A. T. Clay gave us vols. xiv, xv of the *Publications of the Babylonian Expedition of the University of Pennsylvania* (Philadelphia, University of Pennsylvania, 1906), entitled *Documents from the Temple Archives of Nippur, dated in the Reigns of Cassite Rulers*. They showed how the old customs were preserved and modified with fresh immigrations. These were followed in 1912 by *Documents from the Temple Archives of Nippur, dated in the Reigns of Cassite Rulers, the Museum Publications of the Babylonian Section*, vol. ii, no. 2 (Philadelphia Museum), completing the collections. Some of the same sort from Nippur, in the E. A. Hoffmann collection in the Metropolitan Museum in New York, were noted in Radau's *Early Babylonian History*, pp. 328–9 (New York, 1900).

F. E. Peiser, in 1905, had published *Urkunden aus der Zeit der dritten babylonischen Dynastie in Urschrift, Umschrift und Übersetzung, dazu Rechtsausführungen von J. Kohler* (Berlin, Wolf Peiser). These appear to have belonged to a family of Babylonians, some of whom adopted Cassite names. More of the same group found their way to the Berlin Museums, and more are in private hands and in the Louvre.

C. J. Ball contributed to the *Proceedings of the Society of Biblical Archaeology* for 1907, pp. 273–4, *A Kassite Text*.

D. D. Luckenbill in the *American Journal of Semitic Languages and Literatures*, 1907, pp. 280–322, gave a most valuable *Study of the Temple Documents from the Cassite Period*.

The scarcity of legal documents from this period may be estimated from the fact that in *Texte juristischen und geschäftlichen Inhalts* (see p. 81, above) only the so-called boundary-stones could be quoted.

It is in the Third Dynasty of Babylon that the Boundary-Stone or Kudurru inscriptions first appear. These have been much discussed, especially from the side of the curious symbols which occur upon them, often regarded as signs of the Zodiac, or emblems of the gods.

In the *Beiträge zur Assyriologie*, vol. ii, pp. 111–204, a number of such texts were published and partly discussed by C. Belser, as *Babylonische Kudurru-Inschriften*. Peiser incorporated some in the fourth volume of Schrader's *Keilinschriftliche Bibliothek*. W. J. Hinke gave in 1907, as vol. iv of Series D of the *Publications of the Babylonian Expedition of the University of Pennsylvania* (Philadelphia, University of Pennsylvania), *A New Boundary-Stone of Nebuchadrezzar I from Nippur*, in which he also gave a full bibliography of the subject, collected names, words, &c., from all the texts of the sort hitherto published, and discussed the symbols. In *Babylonian Boundary-stones and Memorial Tablets in the British Museum, with an Atlas of Plates* (London, British Museum, 1912), L. W. KING gave the whole of the British Museum material. In 1911 HINKE contributed to the *Semitic Study Series* (Leiden, E. J. Brill) a useful collection in *Selected Babylonian Kudurru Inscriptions.* Many such inscriptions are published by V. SCHEIL with transcriptions and translations in *Mémoires de la Délégation en Perse* (Paris, E. Leroux), vols. ii, pp. 86–94, 97–116; vi, pp. 30–47; vii, 137–53; x, 87–96. F. STEINMETZER contributed *Eine Schenkungsurkunde des Königs Melishichu* to the *Beiträge zur Assyriologie,* vol. viii, pp. 1–38.

HINKE gives an excellent bibliography of the Babylonian *kudurru* inscriptions, their publications, transliterations, translations, and discussions. Some are of the nature of *Freibriefe*, and MEISSNER so treated one in the *Zeitschrift für Assyriologie,* 1889, pp. 259–67, cf. pp. 403–4. He also wrote *Assyrische Freibriefe* in the *Beiträge zur Assyriologie* II. (1894), pp. 565–72, 581–8, giving text, transliteration, translation, and discussion of three examples from the reign of Ashurbanipal and one of Adad-niraris. In my *Assyrian Deeds and Documents* (Cambridge, Deighton, Bell & Co., 1902), nos. 646, 647, 648, and 651, I republished these texts and added nos. 649, 650, two texts of Ashur-etil-ilâni, son and successor of Ashurbanipal, nos. 652, 653, 654, 655, 656 (= 808 in vol. ii) of Adad-nirari, nos. 657, 658 (dated in B.C. 730), 659 (names Tiglath-Pileser), 660 (now joined to other fragments as 809, an important grant by Sargon II in connexion with the site of Dur-Sargon), 661, 662 (?), 663, and possibly also nos. 669, 671, 672, 673, 674 (see now no. 1101), 692 (now part of 807), 714 (now part of 809), and in vol. ii, nos. 734, 735, 736, 737, 738 (?), 739, 740 (?), 741 (?), on to 752, all possible fragments of similar proclamations, *Freibriefe*, charters, or the schedules to them. I have collected the references here, as the texts seem to have met with insufficient attention. WINCKLER had published parts of some of them in his *Altorientalische Forschungen* (Leipzig, E. Pfeiffer, 1898), vol. ii, pp. 4–8, and assigned the Ashur-etil-ilâni texts to Esarhaddon's reign, and in the note on p. 192 to Sin-shar-ishkun. F. E. PEISER made some acute suggestions as to the readings of the text and their meanings.

On no. 809 MEISSNER wrote a full discussion in the *Mitteilungen der Vorderasiatischen Gesellschaft,* 1903, pp. 85–96.

In 1883 H. V. HILPRECHT published *Freibrief Nebukadnezar's I.* (Leipzig, Hinrichs), with great advances on the previous treatment, and published others in *Old Babylonian Inscriptions,* vol. i, part 1 (1893), nos. 80, 83, part 2 (1896), nos. 149, 150. In 1891 K. L. TALLQVIST wrote on

Babylonische Schenkungsbriefe (Helsingfors).   In the *Beiträge zur Assyriologie*, 1894, pp. 258–73, Fr. Delitzsch published and admirably treated *Der Berliner Merodachbaladan-Stein*.

Ed. Cuq in *La Propriété foncière en Chaldée* gave a new view of the meaning of these documents and the significance of their first appearing in the Kassite period.   It will be seen from the titles given in the above works that no complete unanimity prevails as to their nature and purpose.

We may now turn back to the class of texts usually called contracts.

The Assyrian empire has not yielded much of this class of document, before the time of Sargon II, B.C. 785–722.   A number of texts have been reported in the *Mitteilungen der Deutschen Orient-Gesellschaft zu Berlin* as found at Asshur by the German excavators there, which date from times both early and late.   The publication of these texts will doubtless soon be achieved and add greatly to our knowledge.   The treatment in Assyria seems to be largely reminiscent of that of Babylonia under the First Dynasty, but there are wide divergences doubtless due to the foreign elements in the Assyrian population.   We are not yet possessed of sufficient material to assign the changes to their true causes, but we know enough to be sure that they were not on the whole due to contemporary developments in Babylonia.

In *Assyrian Deeds and Documents relating to the transfer of Property*, in three volumes, by C. H. W. Johns, published in 1898–1901 (Deighton, Bell & Co., Cambridge, 3 vols.), practically all the material of this class in the British Museum then catalogued was edited.   These tablets apparently all came from Nineveh.   There are now many more similar tablets in the British Museum listed in the *Supplement to the Catalogue*.   Recently in *Assyrische Rechtsurkunden von J. Kohler und A. Ungnad* (Leipzig, Ed. Pfeiffer, 1913) a series of transliterations and translations have been commenced which will form a key to the whole, including many other texts since published.

It was on these texts that J. Oppert formed his views given in *Das Assyrische Landrecht*, and in *Le droit de retrait lignager à Ninive*, see p. 72.

V. Scheil published in his *Notes d'épigraphie* in the *Recueil de Travaux*, xx, note xl (1898), pp. 202–5, four tablets which possibly did not come from Nineveh.   I republished the texts as nos. 779–82 in my *Deeds and Documents* above.   The first is discussed by Meissner as *Eine assyrische Schenkungsurkunde* in the *Mitteilungen der Vorderasiatischen Gesellschaft*, 1903, pp. 103–5, where he points out that my no. 619 is another like text.   Here Adi-mati-ilu and other property were given to a son who was to take a double portion and divide the rest with his brothers.

F. E. Peiser in the *Orientalistische Litteraturzeitung*, 1905, cols. 130–4, gave *Ein neuer assyrischer Kontrakt*, V. Scheil in the same journal for 1904, col. 70, and in the *Recueil de Travaux*, xxiv, note lxii, p. 24, pointed out others, while in *Vorderasiatische Schriftdenkmäler*, vol. i, nos. 84–111, A. Ungnad published several more from Kannu' and Kerkûk. S. Schiffer discussed many of these as *Keilschriftliche Spuren der in der zweiten Hälfte des 8. Jahrhunderts von den Assyrern nach Mesopotamien deportierten Samarier*, a Beiheft to *Orientalistische Litteraturzeitung* (Berlin, W. Peiser, 1907), with which may be compared an article in the *Proceedings of the Society of Biblical Archaeology*, 1908, pp. 107-15, 137–41, on *The Lost Ten Tribes of Israel*, by C. H. W. Johns. In an article *Aus dem Louvre*, F. E. Peiser published in the *Orientalistische Litteraturzeitung*, 1903, cols. 192–200, a new collation of no. 1,141 in my *Deeds and Documents*, which had been formerly treated by Place, Oppert, and Strassmaier; and an edition of another text of this class. The new *Supplement* to the *Catalogue of the Tablets in the Kouyunjik Collection in the British Museum*, by L. W. King (London, British Museum, 1914), shows that many more such texts await publication, and there are others in the Museums in England and America.

This class of document was early known for the times of the Neo-babylonian Empire, and thousands of the so-called contracts have been published down to the century before the Christian era.

J. Oppert began the task of publishing and deciphering contracts, for which his legal training as well as his philological learning especially fitted him. His work may be gathered from the bibliography in the second volume of the *Beiträge zur Assyriologie*, pp. 523–56. His great effort was *Documents juridiques de l'Assyrie et de la Chaldée* (Paris, Maisonneuve, 1877), but he continued to deal with contracts up to his death. Here as elsewhere comparison of fresh material continually brought new light.

A number of such tablets were copied by T. G. Pinches (?) for the fifth volume of *Inscriptions of Western Asia* (London, British Museum, 1909, plates lxvii, lxviii), on which Oppert built his determination of Babylonian measures. J. N. Strassmaier, in 1855, published *Die babylonischen Inschriften im Museum zu Liverpool nebst anderen aus der Zeit von Nebukadnezar bis Darius* (Leiden, J. Brill).

The tablets in the British Museum from Sippara, Babylon, Borsippa, &c., dated in the reigns of Nebuchadrezzar, Nabopolassar, Evil-Merodach, Neriglissar, Nabonidus, Cyrus, Cambyses, and Darius, were also edited by J. N. Strassmaier as *Babylonische Texte, Inschriften von den Thontafeln des British Museums copiert und autographiert*, in twelve volumes (Leipzig, 1887–1897). On the mass of material thus rendered available to scholars were based a very large number of memoirs and monographs which may be arranged here. K. L. Tallqvist, in 1890, published *Die Sprache der Contracte Nabû-nâ'id's* (Helsingfors, J. C. Frenckell), in which he collected all the words and phrases occurring in these texts, with useful indexes. R. Zehnpfund gave *Babylonische Weberrechnungen* in the *Beiträge zur Assyriologie*, i, pp. 492 ff. (1890): L. Demuth, *Fünfzig Rechts- und Verwaltungsurkunden aus der Zeit des Königs Kyros*, in the same journal, vol. iii, pp. 393–444 (1898); E. ZIEMER, *Fünfzig Rechts- und Verwaltungs-urkunden aus der Zeit des Königs Kambyses*, same volume, pp. 445–92; V. MARX, *Die Stellung der Frauen in Babylonien gemäss den Kontrakten aus der Zeit von Nebukadnezar bis Darius*, same journal, vol. iv, pp. 1–77, 1902; and E. KOTALLA, *Fünfzig babylonische Rechts- und Verwaltungs-urkunden aus der Zeit des Königs Artaxerxes I*, same volume, pp. 551–74. FR. DELITZSCH contributed *Notizen zu den neubabylonischen Kontrakttafeln*, same journal, vol. iii, pp. 385–92 (1898), and J. KOHLER, *Ein Beitrag zum neubabylonischen Recht*, vol. iv, pp. 423–30. F. E. PEISER, in 1889, published *Keilinschriftliche Actenstücke aus babylonischen Städten* (Berlin, W. Peiser), and, in 1890, *Babylonische Verträge des Berliner Museums* (Berlin, W. Peiser). This marked great advances on OPPERT's work, owing to STRASSMAIER's new material and the Berlin collections. He next contributed a selection of transliterations and translations to the fourth volume of SCHRADER's *Keilinschriftliche Bibliothek* (1896), p. 81, above. Then from 1890–1898 appeared *Aus dem babylonischen Rechtsleben* (Leipzig, Pfeiffer), in conjunction with J. KOHLER, containing many new texts. A. B. MOLDENKE, in 1893, published for the Metropolitan Museum at New York a volume of *Cuneiform Texts*, all of this period. In 1890 appeared *Recherches sur quelques contrats babyloniens*, by A. BOISSIER (Paris, E. Leroux).

In the *Zeitschrift für Assyriologie* (Weimar, E. Felber, 1894) Y. LE GAC published *Quelques inscriptions assyro-babyloniennes du Musée Lycklama à Cannes*, pp. 385–90, and in *Babyloniaca* (Paris, P. Geuthner, 1910) *Textes babyloniens de la Collection Lycklama à Cannes*, pp. 33–72. In 1902 T. G. PINCHES contributed to the *Verhandlungen des XIII. Orientalistischen Congresses* some *Notes on a Small Collection of Tablets from the Birs Nimroud belonging to Lord Amherst of Hackney*.

In vols. III–VI of the *Vorderasiatische Schriftdenkmäler* (1907–1908) A. UNGNAD published many texts of this period, and gave later some valuable *Untersuchungen* on the same, *Aus der altbabylonischen Kontrakt-literatur*, to the *Orientalistische Litteraturzeitung*, 1912, cols. 106–8.

A new source for this material was the finds at Nippur, printed in *The Publications of the Babylonian Expedition of the University of Penn-sylvania*, Philadelphia, Series A. *Cuneiform Texts*, vol. viii, part 1 contained *Legal and Commercial Transactions from the Neobabylonian Empire to Darius II*, by A. T. CLAY, 1908; vols. ix and x, by the same author, contained *Business Documents of Murashu Sons of Nippur in the reign of Artaxerxes I* (1898), and *Business Documents in the reign of Darius II* (1904). A new series has since been commenced.

The Museum Publications of the Babylonian Section of the University of Pennsylvania (Philadelphia Museum), vol. ii, no. 1, gives *Business Documents of Murashû Sons, of Nippur*, by A. T. CLAY (1912), and vol. ii, no. 2, *Documents from the Temple Archives at Nippur*, by the same author (1912). *Selected Business Documents of the Neo-Babylonian Period* in the *Semitic*

Study Series, by A. UNGNAD (Leiden, Brill, 1908), forms a useful introduction to the subject.

In 1911 appeared *Hundert ausgewählte Rechtsurkunden aus der Spätzeit des babylonischen Schrifttums von Xerxes bis Mithridates, 485–93 v. Chr.*, by A. UNGNAD and J. KOHLER (Leipzig, Pfeiffer), and I. L. HOLT contributed to the *American Journal of Semitic Languages and Literatures* a study of *some Tablets from the R. C. Thompson Collection in Haskell Oriental Museum, The University of Chicago*.

Of considerable interest as in some senses a link between Babylonia and Palestine are the Cappadocian Tablets. The first notice of them was given by T. G. PINCHES in the *Proceedings of the Society of Biblical Archaeology*, Nov. 1, 1881, pp. 11–18. Some tablets in the British Museum were acquired from a dealer who said they had been found in Cappadocia. The script was then quite unfamiliar, and they were supposed at first to be written in a language neither Sumerian nor Semitic. GOLENISCHEFF published in 1891 the text of twenty-four tablets of the same class which he had acquired at Kaisareyeh. He made out that many words were Assyrian and read many names. FR. DELITZSCH made a most valuable study of them in the *Abhandlungen der philos.-hist. Classe der K. Sächs. Gesellschaft d. Wissenschaften*, 1893, no. 11. In 1894 P. JENSEN in the *Zeitschrift für Assyriologie*, vol. ix, pp. 62–81, made many corrections and additions. F. E. PEISER then discussed them in his introduction to the fourth volume of SCHRADER's *Keilinschriftliche Bibliothek*, and gave the transcription and translation of the texts of nine, pp. 50–56. A considerable number more were discovered at Boghaz Koi, Kara Eyuk, and elsewhere, and published by V. SCHEIL in the *Mémoires de la Mission en Cappadoce*, and commented upon by A. BOISSIER in the *Proceedings of the Society for Biblical Archaeology*, 1900, pp. 106 ff. Four Cappadocian tablets were published by THUREAU-DANGIN among his *Lettres et Contrats*, see p. 82, above.

In *Babyloniaca*, 1908, pp. 1–45, A. H. SAYCE translated the Golenischeff texts, and others published by Chantre, or found by Ramsay, &c.

T. G. PINCHES with A. H. SAYCE published and discussed *The Cappadocian Tablet from Yuzghat in the Liverpool Institute of Archaeology*, 1906.

In 1908 T. G. PINCHES published twenty more in the *Annals of Archaeology of the Liverpool University*, vol. i, pp. 49–80. In the *Florilegium de Vogüé*, pp. 591–k, THUREAU-DANGIN discussed *Un acte de répudiation sur une tablette cappadocienne*, 1909, and in the *Revue d'Assyriologie*, 1911, pp. 142–51, gave more texts fixing *La date des tablettes cappadociennes* as contemporary with the *Dynasty of Ur* in Babylonia, thus proving cuneiform to have been widely used in that region to write a Semitic language long before the time of Hammurabi. In *Babyloniaca*, 1911, pp. 65–80, A. H. SAYCE gave some *Cappadocian Cuneiform Tablets from Kara Eyuk*, affiliating them with early Assyrian rulers. In the same journal, 1911, pp. 216–28, A. BOISSIER gave more texts under the title *Nouveaux documents de Boghaz Köi*. In the same journal, 1912, pp. 182–93, A. H. SAYCE wrote upon *The Cappadocian Cuneiform Tablets of the University of Pennsylvania.*

All these works have contributed comments of more or less value, and the whole point to a close connexion with Babylonia and Assyria, and the extended use of cuneiform in Cappadocia from very early times, whence it was doubtless taken over by the later Hittites.

BABYLONIAN AND ASSYRIAN LETTERS.

A very large number of letters have been preserved to us from all periods of Babylonian and Assyrian history. Many of them are addressed to private correspondents, and concern matters of everyday life. They are often most obscure, as they assume so much knowledge on the part of the recipient which is withheld from us. Where we can grasp their reference they furnish considerable light upon social conditions.

A large number, however, are royal letters or dispatches from the king and his officers to subordinates, or *vice versa*. These more often concern public affairs.

As yet few letters have come down to us which we can date before the First Dynasty of Babylon, but some will be found in the *Inventaire des tablettes de Tello* (see p. 80), and among the various publications of Temple accounts and contracts, as early as the times of Sargon of Akkad.

In the *Beiträge zur Assyriologie*, vol. ii, pp. 557–64, 572–9, MEISSNER published *Altbabylonische Briefe* (1893), with discussions.

In the times of Hammurabi, or the First Dynasty of Babylon, our sources for epistolary correspondence become very ample. L. W. KING in his magnificent work, *The Letters and Inscriptions of Hammurabi, King of Babylon, about B.C. 2200 ; to which is added a series of letters of other Kings of the First Dynasty of Babylon* (vol. i, *Introduction and Babylonian Texts* ; vol. ii, *Babylonian Texts*, continued ; vol. iii, *English Translation, Commentary, Vocabularies, Introduction, etc.*, London, Luzac & Co., 1898), gave a complete edition of these letters. The materials for history and social life were epoch-making. In the *Beiträge zur Assyriologie* G. NAGEL translated a number of these texts, *Briefe Hammurabi's an Sin-iddinam*, vol. iv, pp. 434–83, to which FR. DELITZSCH added *Zusatzbemerkungen*, pp. 483–500. He, with J. A. KNUDTZON, wrote on the same subject, vol. iv, pp. 88–100. M. W. MONTGOMERY took *Briefe aus der Zeit des babylonischen Königs Hammurabi* as subject for her doctor's dissertation (Leipzig, Pries, 1901). A. KLOSTERMANN published *Ein diplomatischer Briefwechsel aus dem 2. Jahrtausend v. Chr.* (Leipzig, Deichert, 1903). C. V. GELDEREN contributed *Ausgewählte babylonisch-assyrische Briefe* to the *Beiträge zur Assyriologie*, iv, 1902, pp. 501–45. Another great collection was published by THUREAU-DANGIN in *Lettres et contrats de l'époque de la première dynastie babylonienne* (Paris, P. Geuthner, 1910). The author transliterated, translated, and commented upon three of these texts as *Lettres de l'époque de la première dynastie babylonienne* in *The Hilprecht Anniversary Volume*, pp. 156–63.

Les Lettres de Hammurapi à Sin-idinnam, transcription, traduction et commentaire, précédées d'une étude sur deux caractères du style assyro-babylonien, by F. C. JEAN (Paris, J. Gabalda, 1913), gives an idea of the subject.

P. S. LANDERSDORFER, in 1908, had edited *Altbabylonische Privatbriefe, transkribiert, übersetzt und kommentiert, nebst einer Einleitung und 4 Registern* (Paderborn, Schonigh), and G. A. BARTON gave an article *On an old Babylonian Letter addressed to Lushtamar* in the *Journal of the American Oriental Society*, pp. 220–22.

A. SCHOLLMEYER wrote on *Altbabylonische Privatbriefe* in *Babyloniaca,* vi, pp. 57–64, 1912, and in 1911 published *Neuveröffentlichte altbabylonische Briefe und ihre Bedeutung für die Kultur des Orients : Sechs Vorträge vor der Hildesheimer Generalversammlung* (Köln, P. Bachem).

E. EBELING contributed to the *Revue d'Assyriologie*, 1913, pp. 15 ff., 105–56, articles on *Altbabylonische Briefe*. *The First Letter of Rim-Sin, King of Larsa,* was published by ST. LANGDON in the *Proceedings of the Society for Biblical Archaeology*, 1911, pp. 221–2.

The period of the Third or Kassite Dynasty has not yet yielded much.

H. RADAU made as much as possible out of a number of fragments found at Nippur in vol. xvii, 1 of Series A of *The Publications of the Babylonian Expedition of the University of Pennsylvania* called *Letters to Cassite Kings from the Temple Archives of Nippur* (1908).

Very little more is known of Epistolary Literature till we reach the Sargonide Dynasty in Assyria. With the Library of Ashurbanipal at Nineveh were found a large number of letters and dispatches, alike royal, public and private, Assyrian and Neobabylonian, which early attracted notice. S. A. SMITH published a number from the collections in the British Museum in his *Assyrian Letters from the Royal Library at Nineveh, transcribed, translated, and explained* (Leipzig, Pfeiffer, 1887–1888), and in *Miscellaneous Assyrian Texts of the British Museum with Textual Notes* (Leipzig, Pfeiffer, 1887), besides a series of articles in the *Proceedings of the Society of Biblical Archaeology* for 1887–1888 called *Assyrian Letters.*

The present writer dealt with *Sennacherib's Letters to his Father Sargon,* in the *Proceedings of the Society of Biblical Archaeology*, 1895, pp. 220–39. FR. DELITZSCH in the *Beiträge zur Assyriologie*, vol. i, pp. 185-248, 613–31, and vol. ii, pp. 19–62, under the title *Zur assyrisch-babylonischen Briefliteratur,* laid deep the foundations of the study of letters, editing many fresh texts (1890–1894). H. WINCKLER published a large number of letters in his *Sammlung von Keilschrifttexten* (Leipzig, Pfeiffer, 1894). T. G. PINCHES published *Zwei assyrische Briefe* (Leipzig, Pfeiffer, 1887).

R. F. HARPER has continued to edit the *Assyrian and Babylonian Letters belonging to the Kouyunjik Collections of the British Museum,* vol. i, 1892 ; vol. ii, 1893 ; vol. iii, 1896 ; vol. iv, 1896 ; vol. v, 1900 ; vol. vi, 1902 ;

vol. vii, 1902 ; vol. viii, 1902 ; vol. ix, 1909 ; vol. x, 1911 ; vol. xi, 1911 ; vol. xii, 1913 ; vol. xiii, 1913 (Chicago University Press; Luzac & Co., London), which will contain all the British Museum collections from Nineveh. These copies have been made with the greatest care, and constitute the chief source of this material up to the present time. Numerous works have been built upon them as foundation. CHRISTOPHER JOHNSTON wrote on *The Epistolary Literature of the Assyrians and Babylonians* (Baltimore, 1898), reprinted from *Journal of the American Oriental Society*. E. BEHRENS published in 1906 his *Assyrisch-babylonische Briefe kultischen Inhalts aus der Sargonidenzeit* (Leipzig, Pries, 1905). LEHMANN-HAUPT gave *Zwei unveröffentlichte Keilschrifttexte* in *Hilprecht Anniversary Volume* (1909), pp. 256–8.

In 1910 came M. ZEITLIN's *Le style administratif chez les Assyriens ; choix de lettres assyriennes et babyloniennes, transcrites, traduites et accompagnées de notes* (Paris, Geuthner). In the *Zeitschrift für Assyriologie* C. BEZOLD gave *Zwei assyrische Berichte* (vol. xxvi, 1912, p. 114–25).

In 1911, E. G. KLAUBER wrote *Zur babylonisch-assyrischen Briefliteratur* in *Babyloniaca*, iv, pp. 180–86 ; and in 1912 *Zur Politik und Kultur der Sargonidenzeit : Untersuchungen auf Grund der Brieftexte* in the January and July numbers of vol. xxviii of the *American Journal of Semitic Languages and Literatures*. In the January number of this volume also appeared L. WATERMAN's *Textual Notes on the Letters of the Sargon Period*. A most valuable contribution to an obscure period of Ashurbanipal's reign was made by H. H. FIGULLA, *Der Briefwechsel Bélibni's : Historische Urkunden aus der Zeit Asurbanipals*, in *Mitteilungen der Vorderasiatischen Gesellschaft* (Leipzig, Hinrichs, 1912). E. G. KLAUBER, in 1910, published *Assyrisches Beamtentum nach Briefen aus der Sargonidenzeit* (Leipzig, Hinrichs), and in *Der alte Orient*, xii, Heft 2, *Keilschriftbriefe : Staat und Gesellschaft in der babylonisch-assyrischen Briefliteratur* (Leipzig, Hinrichs, 1911). V. SCHEIL under the title *Diplomatica* dealt with similar texts in the *Hilprecht Anniversary Volume*, pp. 873 ff.

Letters of the Neo-Babylonian period are numerous but not much published. R. C. THOMPSON published *Late Babylonian Letters* (London, Luzac & Co., 1906) with translations, &c. FR. MARTIN gave *Lettres néo-babyloniennes* (Paris, Champion, 1909), and *Trois lettres néo-babyloniennes* in the *Hilprecht Anniversary Volume*, 1909. In the *Proceedings of the Society of Biblical Archaeology*, 1911, pp. 157–8, T. G. PINCHES published *Two late Babylonian Letters*.

NOTES

[1] This, at any rate, is usually stated on the authority of the monkish chroniclers. J. R. GREEN in *A Short History of the English People* (London, Macmillan, 1875), p. 46, records that the Ten Commandments and a portion of the Law of Moses were prefixed to the code drawn up by Alfred and so became part of the law of the land. Whether this ancient tradition will survive modern criticism remains to be seen. The tradition at any rate continues to command widespread credence.

[2] It has been pointed out that references to a particular edition would be out of place here, but for elementary students one may refer to *Ancient Law, its connexion with the early history of society and its relation to modern ideas* (London, G. Routledge and Sons). The many references given in the bibliography to various ancient legislations will suffice for our comparisons, but articles in the *Encyclopædia Britannica* or the *Encyclopædia of Religion and Ethics* may be consulted for further study.

[3] So I was informed by the late Professor Maitland, but I have unfortunately lost the reference he gave me.

[4] In the *Beiträge zur Assyriologie*, 1902, p. 86.

[5] Wednesday, Oct. 29, 1902.

[6] *The Laws of Moses and the Code of Hammurabi* (London, A. & C. Black, 1903).

[7] See on the racial character of the Sumerians, L. W. KING's *Sumer and Akkad, passim,* and the references there.

P. 2, notes 7, 8, 9, see *Survey of Bibliography, Anticipations,* p. 65.

[10] But this work may have to be done when the data exist for recognizing the Sumerian Elements, cf. p. 76 and references to Sumerian Law in the Index.

[11] The Code must have been drawn up later than the conquest of Rim-Sin, or rather its present redaction must. The date was discussed by KING, SCHORR and E. MEYER as well as WINCKLER, most lately by E. CUQ, see *Comptes rendus de l'Académie des Inscriptions et Belles-Lettres,* Jan. 1912, p. 5.

[12] Most recently in *Ancient Babylonia,* by C. H. W. JOHNS (Cambridge, University Press, 1913) pp. 76–80.

[13] See under these names in *Index and Bibliography.*

[14] See p. 67.

[15] See p. 74.

[16] See p. 74

INDEX

Votary, 60, 61, 72.
Vowed women, 6, 60, 61.

Warka, 80.
West Goths, 53.

William the Conqueror, 32.
Wineshops, 60.
Witchcraft, 6.
Women, 1, 5.

AUTHORS MENTIONED

Allotte de la Fuÿe, 79, 80.
Arnold, W. R., 77.

Ball, C. J., 83.
Barton, G. A., 77, 78, 90.
Behrens, E., 91.
Belser, C., 83.
Bezold, C., 91.
Boissier, A., 87, 88.
Bonfante, P., 68.
Boscawen, W. St. Chad, 68, v.

Clay, A. T., 76, 79, 83, 87.
Cohn, G., 53, 72.
Combe, E., 9, 74.
Cook, S. A., 23, 47, 53, 73, 76, v.
Cruveilhier, P., 70.
Cuq, E., 72, 74, 85.

Daiches, S., 69, 72, 74.
Dareste, R., 8, 71, 72.
Davies, W. W., 69.
Deimel, A., 66, 78.
Delaporte, L., 78.
Delitzsch, Fr., 2, 65, 73, 75, 85, 87, 88, 89, 90, v.
De Morgan, J., 1.
Demuth, L., 86.
Dhorme, P., 72, 79.
Driver, S. R., 50.
Dykes, D. O., 70.

Ebeling, E., 90.
Edwards, C., 68.

Fehr, H., 72.
Figulla, H. H., 91.
Freund, L., 73.
Friedrich, Th., 81.

Gautier, J. E., 82.
Gelderen, C. V., 89.
Genouillac, H. de, 77, 78, 79, 80.
Golenischeff, Fr., 88.
Grimme, H., 53.

Harper, R. F., 66, 70, 90, v.
Haupt, P., 75, 76.
Hilprecht, H. V., 74, 77, 84.
Hinke, W. J., 83, 84.
Hobhouse, L. T., 70.
Holt, I. L., 88.
Hommel, F., 9, 75.

Huber, E., 79.
Hussey, M. J., 79.

Jean, F. C., 90.
Jelitto, J., 72.
Jensen, P., 88.
Jeremias, A., 20, 76.
Jhering, R. von, iii, n. 3.
Johns, C. H. W., 68, 69, 70, 74, 84, 85, 86, 90, iv, v.
Johnston, Chr., 91.

Keiser, C. E., 83.
Kent, C. F., 24, 25, 26, 37, 68, 71.
King, L. W., 76, 77, 84, 86, 89, n. 11.
Klauber, E. G., 91.
Klostermann, A., 89.
Knudtzon, J. A., 89.
Kohler, J., 4, 9, 14, 67, 72, 73, 75, 85, 87, 88.
König, E., 70.
Koschaker, P., 73.
Kotalla, E., 87.

Landersdorfer, P. S., 90.
Langdon, St., 66, 78, 79, 83, 90.
Lau, R. J., 77.
Layard, A. H., 80.
Le Gac, Y., 87.
Lehmann (Haupt), C. F., 70, 91.
Likhatscheff, N. P., 79.
Lightfoot, J., 15.
Littmann, E., 74.
Loftus, W. K., 80.
Lotichius, P., 70.
Luckenbill, D. D., 83.
Lyon, D. G., 26, 27, 70, 71.

MacAlister?, 22.
Maine, Sir H., 6.
Moldenke, A. B., 87.
Mari, Fr., 68.
Martin, Fr., 91.
Marx, V., 73, 87.
Meissner, Br., 2, 4, 65, 71, 73, 75, 81, 84, 85, 89.
Mercer, S. A. B., 73.
Mommsen, Th., 72.
Montgomery, M. W., 89.
Müller, D. H., 9, 15, 50, 53, 67, 68, 69, 70, 71, 73, xiii.

BABYLONIAN WORDS

amêlu, 7, 74.
dinâni, 2.
gallabu, 12.
kânu, 8.
kittu, 1.
kudurru, 83.
mishâru, 1.

mâr banûtu, 12.
mash-en-kak, 8.
mushkênu, 8, 9, 46, 74.
nibûtu, 42.
ninu Anum tsirum, 2.
rîd tsâbê, 74.
wardu, 7, 10.

www.ingramcontent.com/pod-product-compliance
Lightning Source LLC
Chambersburg PA
CBHW071143090426
42736CB00012B/2212